OXFORD &
THE COTSWOLDS

TOP SIGHTS · LOCAL EXPERIENCES

GREG WARD

Contents

Plan Your Trip

Bodleian Library (p40)
NICK HUGHES / NICKHDESIGN / 500PX ©

Welcome to Oxford & the Cotswolds

With its ancient colleges, and alleyways lined with pubs and cafes, the university town of Oxford offers a seductive blend of history and modern charm. Off to the west, the golden villages, thatched cottages and stately churches of the Cotswolds – little changed since the Middle Ages – encapsulate a timeless rural idyll.

View of Oxford from South Park
JOHN ALEXANDER / GETTY IMAGES ©

Top Sights

Christ Church

Oxford's largest and grandest college **p36**

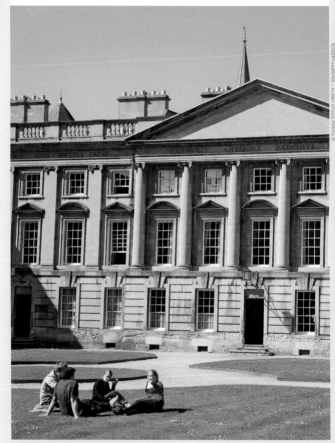

Bodleian Library

Oxford University's magnificent medieval library. **p40**

Blenheim Palace

Baroque extravaganza with glorious gardens **p92**

Magdalen College

Magnificent college with beautiful grounds. **p66**

Pitt Rivers Museum

Eye-opening anthropological oddities. **p80**

Ashmolean Museum

World-class art and archaeology museum **p78**

Chipping Norton

Handsome hilltop town **p97**

Chipping Campden

The perfect golden-hued Cotswolds village **p107**

Stratford-upon-Avon
Historic birthplace of William Shakespeare **p112**

Broadway
Gold-hued cottages and art galleries **p115**

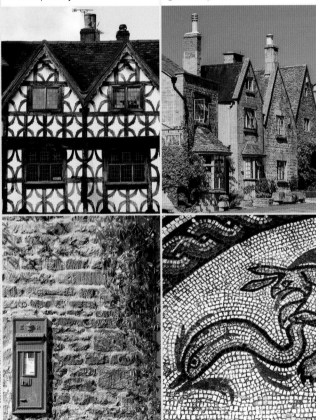

LEFT: OVERSNAP / GETTY IMAGES ©; RIGHT: DAVID HUGHES / SHUTTERSTOCK ©

LEFT: CHRISAPPPS / SHUTTERSTOCK ©; RIGHT: NEIL HOLMES / GETTY IMAGES ©

Burford
Picturesque town with centuries-old church **p126**

Cirencester
Ancient Roman city turned lively Cotswolds town **p136**

Eating

While the Cotswolds villages offer visitors abundant fine dining, Oxford's restaurants tend to be geared towards hungry students, charging reasonable prices for high-quality food. Take your pick from the appealing cafes of central Oxford, the lively neighbourhood gastropubs, and the student-oriented diners along Cowley Rd.

Dining in the Cotswolds

The Cotswolds having become renowned for a sustainable, locally sourced approach to cooking, its ravishing villages and sumptuous countryside hold some truly fabulous places to eat. Organic produce, seasonal ingredients and farm-to-table cooking characterise everything from delectable cafe breakfasts and gastropub feasts to Michelin-starred delights. You'll find organic delis, farmers markets and oh-so-English tearooms at every turn. It's always advisable to book ahead, especially for upmarket restaurants but also for the best-known pubs, which attract diners from miles around.

A World Tour of Oxford

Mastering the world's languages and literature can safely be left to Oxford's high-minded students. For visitors, it's more appetising to make a globe-spanning tour of its well-priced international-flavoured restaurants. In the Cowley Road neighbourhood, in particular, almost every major world cuisine is represented, along with some you may have never tried or even heard of. The top of any list has to be the cornucopia of Caribbean specialities at Spiced Roots, while nearby alternatives include Sri Lankan, Slovakian and Moroccan options.

Best in Oxford

Magdalen Arms Relax over a steak pie built for two in Oxford's finest gastropub. (p71)

Spiced Roots Dedicated vegetarians and die-hard carnivores will be blown

BEATS1 / SHUTTERSTOCK ©

away by this Caribbean stunner. (p70)

Edamamé Well-priced specials keep loyal customers returning to this much-loved Japanese cafe. (p52)

Vaults & Garden Wholesome vegetarian and meat-based dishes, overlooked by the stunning Radcliffe Camera. (p53)

Turl Street Kitchen Laidback local bistro with something to suit any time of day. (p53)

Covered Market Central hideaway that's perfect for everything from a pad Thai to a pork pie. (p53)

Best of the Cotswolds

Wheatsheaf The seasonal menus at Northleach's ivy-clad coaching inn deserve their sky-high reputation. (p129)

5 North St Gourmet France-meets-the-Cotswolds tasting menus in Winchcombe, with ample vegetarian choices. (p123)

Wild Thyme Up-to-the-minute British cuisine, especially fresh Cotswolds meats, in Chipping Norton. (p99)

Badgers Hall The perfect Cotswolds tearoom offers wonderful fresh-baked delights. (p111)

Mount Inn This irresistible hilltop pub, near Broadway, serves a hearty British menu with fabulous local cheeses. (p121)

Best World Food in Oxford

Spiced Roots Goat curry, jerk chicken, oxtail stew – Caribbean cuisine at its consummate best. (p70)

Edamamé Savour Japanese specialities – though seldom sushi – amid lunchtime's crowd of enthusiastic students. (p52)

Oli's Thai Join in-the-know locals for some of the tastiest Thai cooking you'll ever encounter. (p71)

Coconut Tree Sri Lankan street snacks, including delicious 'hoppers', served in tapas-sized portions. (p72)

Al-Shami Lebanese favourite, up in Jericho, that's a sure-fire winner for every palate. (p85)

Drinking

Savouring a pint in a traditional English pub ranks among the great joys of visiting Oxford and the Cotswolds. Every Cotswolds village holds at least one glorious old inn, while Oxford boasts countless classic pubs. Many in the centre and Jericho reverberate with literary associations, while Cowley Rd holds a fine crop of lively modern bars.

An Oxford Pub Crawl

With atmospheric pubs squeezing into every nook and cranny, central Oxford is perfect for a pub crawl. While the pick of the crop, the legendary, labyrinthine Turf Tavern, is buried in a back alleyway, the main concentrations are along or off the east–west George St/Broad St axis, and south along St Aldate's. You may not see as many undergraduates as you might imagine – they prefer to drink in their college bars.

Gourmet Gastropubs

In the Cotswolds much of the finest food can be found in veteran village pubs that double as high-class restaurants. Oxford's acclaimed gastropubs, too, are a real treat, where you can wash down a great meal with a pint of finest ale. While not every Oxford pub serves good food – in fact few of the city-centre pubs do – it's a different story in residential neighbourhoods like Jericho.

Best Oxford Pubs

Turf Tavern This glorious old pub, rich in real ales, is a medieval maze of corridors and hideaways. (p56)

Lamb & Flag Writers including JRR Tolkien, CS Lewis and Thomas Hardy found inspiration for their fabulous alternate universes – along, of course, with beer – in this historic pub. (p87)

Head of the River A broad riverside terrace renders this imposing pub perfect for a sunset pint. (pictured; p56)

The Perch The ideal destination for a summer stroll, with its verdant Thames-side garden. (p91)

CHRISDORNEY / SHUTTERSTOCK ©

Best Cotswolds Pubs

Crown & Trumpet Local real ales and ciders flow in abundance in this welcoming Broadway inn. (p117)

Woolpack Inn Author Laurie Lee was a long-time regular at this village pub, just south of Painswick. (p141)

King's Head Inn Blissfully rural 16th-century cider house, set amid lovely gardens outside Stow-on-the-Wold. (p104)

Old Crown Inn Time-honoured village pub, facing Uley's village green, and serving locally brewed beer. (p143)

Eight Bells Inn Cosy centuries-old pub, famous for its food, in the heart of Chipping Campden. (p111)

Best Oxford Gastropubs

Magdalen Arms Oxford's finest gastropub can match any restaurant in the city, or the whole of England for that matter. (p71)

Old Bookbinders Ale House A gastropub with a Gallic twist, specialising in French cuisine in general and savoury crêpes in particular. (p84)

The Chester Backstreet pub that serves a memorable roast lunch on Sundays, and a huge steak platter the rest of the week. (p72)

Rickety Press The burgers and pizzas in this Jericho favourite way exceed the usual expectations. (p85)

Worth A Trip

Half the fun of the lovely, riverside **Isis Farmhouse** (☎01865-243854; www.theisisfarmhouse.co.uk; Haystacks Corner, The Towing Path, Iffley Lock; ⊙noon-9pm Mon, to 11pm Thu, to midnight Fri, 10am-midnight Sat, to 10pm Sun) – yes, it really is a farmhouse – is the half-hour walk from Central Oxford to get there, south along the Thames footpath from Folly Bridge. The other half is drinking fine local beers in its rustic garden. And the third half is the live jazz on Sunday afternoons.

Activities

Apart from punting or rowing – a crucial component of any Oxford education – your main activity will probably be walking. Expect to do a lot, exploring Oxford itself and heading into the countryside in search of scenery and rural pubs. Further afield, the gentle hills of the Cotswolds are perfect for walking, cycling and horse riding.

Messing About on the River

Whiling away languid days on the river – or, as Oxford-educated writer Kenneth Grahame put it in *The Wind in the Willows*, 'messing about in boats' – is what an Oxford summer is for.

Punting is all about lounging back in a flat-bottomed boat, sipping a cooling glass of Pimms as the city's glorious architecture glides by. To achieve that blissful state, you must first master punting's greatest skill – persuading someone else to do all the hard work.

The act of punting, propelling a boat along a river by repeatedly poking a long pole into the muddy bottom, is far more difficult than it appears. If you just want to relax, consider paying for a guided tour instead. Most punts hold five people, four sprawled on cushions plus the punter standing at the back. Go-it-alone punt rental costs between £17 and £22 per hour, and operators usually charge a full day's rental as a refundable deposit.

Walking in the Cotswolds

The 102-mile **Cotswold Way** (www.nationaltrail.co.uk/cotswold-way) gives a wonderful overview of the region. Meandering from Chipping Campden in the northeast to Bath in the southwest, it passes through lovely countryside, linking ancient sites and tiny villages, with no major climbs or difficult stretches. It's readily accessible from many points en route, if you fancy tackling a shorter section or

ARSTY / GETTY IMAGES ©

a circular walk from your village of choice.

Other long-distance trails that pass through the Cotswolds include the 100-mile **Gloucestershire Way**, from Chepstow to Tewkesbury via Stow-on-the-Wold; the 55-mile **St Kenelm's Way** into Worcestershire; and the 184-mile **Thames Path** (www.national trail.co.uk/thames-path), which tracks from just southwest of Cirencester all the way to London.

Local tourist offices sell walking maps and advise on routes.

Best Oxford River Activities

Magdalen Bridge Boathouse Don't leave without taking a punt at punting, but just be aware – you're going to get wet. (p69)

Cherwell Boathouse If you'd prefer to punt away from prying eyes, head to this idyllic upstream spot. (pictured; p88)

Salter Bros Rent a punt, rowing boat or motor boats from the same company Lewis Carroll used for the picnic that gave the world Alice in Wonderland. (p56)

Eights Week We can't all be champion rowers, but we can all watch Oxford's proudest sporting tradition, held in May each year.

Best Oxford Walks

Magdalen College Wandering these woods and meadows, you can't believe you're still in Oxford. (p66)

Christ Church Meadow Footpaths through this open parkland run beside both the Thames and the Cherwell. (p39)

Port Meadow Perfect for a riverside walk from Jericho, this marshy tract is a haven for rare plants. (p90)

Isis Farmhouse You can only reach this riverside pub via a half-hour walk on the Thames path. (p13)

Botanic Garden Serious scientific resource it may be, but this riverside garden is also just plain gorgeous. (p69)

Architecture

Oxford centres on a glorious ensemble of honey-coloured historic buildings. The city itself is the real spectacle, but the domed and glowing Radcliffe Camera, and masterpieces by Sir Christopher Wren and Nicholas Hawksmoor, stand out. Pleasures in the Cotswolds are lower-key, but many villages are showcases of golden-hued stone.

Wool Churches of the Cotswolds

The Cotswolds owes its wealth, and its exquisite architecture, to the medieval wool trade. At its peak, between the 13th and 16th centuries, 'Cotswold Lion' sheep were prized across Europe. Beautiful churches, built on the riches from that era, are dotted throughout the region. Almost every town and village boasts its own so-called 'wool church', typically featuring a soaring Perpendicular Gothic tower, fine stained-glass windows and an elaborately carved interior.

Best Cotswolds Wool Churches

St John the Baptist's Church Cirencester's central church is famed for its mighty tower and superb vaulting. (p137)

St John the Baptist's Church Burford's riverside church holds the fascinating Tanfield tomb, and has medieval almshouses alongside. (p127)

St James' Church With its monuments and almshouses, this Chipping Campden landmark is a very grand affair. (p109)

Church of St Peter & St Paul A consummate expression of the distinct Perpendicular Gothic style, in Northleach. (p129)

St Mary's Church Chipping Norton's definitive wool church bursts with intriguing detail, including Green Men. (p99)

Best University Buildings

Radcliffe Camera Oxford's much-loved central landmark is an absolute Palladian gem, surmounted by an elegant dome. (pictured; p42)

Bodleian Library Architectural highlights here include the Gothic, 600-year-old Divinity School and Duke Humfrey's sumptuously decorated Library. (p40)

APEXPHOTOS / GETTY IMAGES ©

Oxford University Museum of Natural History It's worth visiting this charming museum simply to admire its light-filled, glass-roofed Victorian Gothic home. (p84)

Trinity College Besides its beautifully restored Baroque chapel, Trinity can boast Sir Christopher Wren's lovely garden quad. (p49)

New College An especially fine evocation of how Oxford's colleges must have looked during the Middle Ages. (p46)

Magdalen College With its 15th-century tower and idyllic cloisters adorned with fabulous grotesques, Magdalen is simply irresistible. (p66)

All Souls College The pseudo-Gothic towers surveying All Souls' North Quad were the 1710 handiwork of Nicholas Hawksmoor. (p48)

Sheldonian Theatre Modelled on a classical theatre, Sir Christopher Wren's debut work holds an astonishingly intricate ceiling. (p51)

Best Cotswolds Secular Architecture

Arlington Row These splendid cottages adorn Bibury, hailed by William Morris as the most beautiful village in England. (p130)

Sudeley Castle Stunning castle, outside Winchcombe, that sits amid equally resplendent gardens and boasts its own Perpendicular Gothic church. (p122)

Chastleton House An intact Jacobean house, near Chipping Norton, that has the feel of an early-Stuart time capsule. (p99)

Market Hall Open to the breezes, Chipping Campden's tiny honey-coloured market building epitomises the vernacular charms of the Cotswolds. (p109)

Stanway House Medieval manor house, 4 miles from Winchcombe, that's home to Britain's tallest fountain. (p119)

Grevel House Gargoyles still survey Chipping Campden from atop the 650-year-old house of a wealthy wool merchant. (p109)

For Kids

Thanks to its small size and relaxed atmosphere, Oxford is an easy place to explore with kids. Besides holding great family-friendly museums, it offers the irresistible prospect of punting on the river. And even if the colleges might seem a bit dry and serious, several have the huge advantage of having featured in the Harry Potter movies.

Oxford, City of Dreams

The city of dreaming spires has an extraordinary record for inspiring dreamers to create classics of children's literature. Visionary local authors seem to specialize in epic works of fantasy, imbued with otherworldly qualities yet echoing throughout with familiar Oxford scenes.

Christ Church don Lewis Carroll came first, spinning the tales of *Alice In Wonderland* and *Through the Looking Glass*. Almost a century later, JRR Tolkien of Merton College and CS Lewis of Magdalen College would meet weekly in the *Eagle & Child*, and regale each other with the sagas that became *The Lord of the Rings* and *The Chronicles of Narnia* respectively.

Having already produced one trilogy built around alternative versions of Oxford, *His Dark Materials*, novelist Philip Pullman is well into another, *The Book of Dust*, while *Wind in the Willows* author Kenneth Grahame first came to love 'messing about on the river' as a schoolboy in Oxford. Even Dr Seuss (Theodore Geisel) was here, studying literature at Lincoln College.

Best Sights for Kids

Story Museum Storytelling sessions honouring children's books from around the world, especially Oxford's own *Alice in Wonderland*. (p48)

Pitt Rivers Museum Older children will love the bizarre and eye-popping oddities in this eccentric museum. (p80)

Oxford University Museum of Natural History Watch your kids make a beeline for the brontosaurus and other dentally over-privileged

TPX / AGE FOTOSTOCK ©

dinosaurs. (Insect display pictured; p84)

Oxford Castle and Prison Few kids can resist an ancient castle, especially one with a dungeon. (p46)

Bill Spectre's Oxford Ghost Trail These ghost tours are an after-dark treat, assuming your children don't mind being spooked. (p23)

Thirsty Meeples Drop by Oxford's board-games cafe, and your kids won't want to leave. (p57)

Best Harry Potter Locations

Bodleian Library Duke Humfrey's Library doubled as Hogwarts' library, while the Divinity School served as its infirmary. (p40)

Christ Church The magnificent Great Hall, lined with portraits, was re-created to become Hogwarts' dining room. (p36)

New College Beneath the oak tree in the 15th-century cloisters, Draco Malfoy was turned into a ferret. (p46)

Footprints Tours To learn the full story of Harry Potter and Oxford, take a walking tour. (p23)

Best Alice in Wonderland Locations

Christ Church Lewis Carroll lived on one side of Tom Quad, Alice Liddell on the other. (p36)

Salter Bros Carroll took Alice on their fateful river trip in a rowing boat rented here. (p56)

Godstow Nunnery And this is where they stopped for a picnic, and Carroll told his tale. (p91)

Alice's Shop The very shop from *Through the Looking-Glass*, sadly no longer run by a bespectacled sheep. (p61)

Oxford University Museum of Natural History Home to the celebrated Dodo, and lots of other Alice-related creatures. (p84)

Festivals & Events

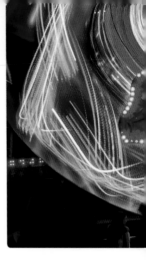

Oxford's busy calendar ranges from high-minded, university-sponsored musical and literary events to assorted student silliness, along with annual fairs dating back to the Middle Ages. The villages of the Cotswolds have their own time-honoured traditions, while the region also hosts a handful of large-scale music festivals.

Best Oxford Music Festivals

Oxford Chamber Music Festival (www.ocmf.net; ☺early Oct) Four days of top-quality concerts across the city.

Common People Oxford (http://oxford.com monpeople.net; South Park; £35 per day, £67.50 weekend; ☺late May) Three-day extravaganza in South Park.

Oxford May Music (☎01865-273323; www.oxfordmaymusic.co.uk; St John the Evangelist Church, 169 Iffley Rd; ☺early May) Unusual festival that combines cutting-edge scientific lectures with classical concerts.

Best Annual Oxford Events

Christmas Light Festival (www.oxfordschristmas.com; Broad St; ☺mid-Nov; 👪) Three-day spree after Oxford's Christmas Lights are switched on.

Oxford Pride (www.oxford-pride.org.uk; Oxford Castle Quarter, Castle St; ☺1st weekend in Jun) Oxford's 10-day LGBT celebration culminates in a city-centre parade.

Cowley Road Carnival (www.cowleyroadcarnival.co.uk; Cowley Rd; ☺1st Sun in Jul) Costumed revellers throng the streets, musicians perform on 30 stages, and stalls sell enticing goodies.

May Morning (☺1 May) At 6am on May Day, a choir sings *Hymnus Eucharisticus* atop Magdalen's belltower, hailed by hard-drinking students gathered on Magdalen Bridge. Morris dancers and bagpipers then caper through the city.

St Giles' Fair (pictured; www.oxford.gov.uk; St Giles; ☺Sep; 👪) Oxford's oldest festival, first celebrated in 1625, honours the feast of St Giles with stalls, rides and funfair attractions.

Best Literary Festivals

Oxford Literary Festival (☎03336-663366; www.oxfordliteraryfestival.org; Worcester College, 1 Walton St; ☺mid-Mar) Across two weekends, and featuring big-name

STANISLAV HALCIN / ALAMY STOCK PHOTO ©

authors, with major events at the Sheldonian Theatre.

Chipping Norton Literary Festival (☏01608-642350; www.chiplitfest.com; ⏱late Apr) Over four days, authors and book-lovers gather for talks, work-shops and competitions.

Best Food & Drink Festivals

Big Feastival (www.the bigfeastival.com; Churchill Heath Farm, Kingman; day tickets £64, weekend camp-ing tickets £179.50; ⏱late Aug; 🚼) Family-oriented festival, on the Cotswolds organic farm where Blur bassist Alex James makes cheese. Chefs and food producers run stalls and restaurants, while the likes

of Madness provide the soundtrack.

Oxford Beer & Cider Festival (www.oxfordbeer festival.camra.org.uk; Town Hall, St Aldate's; ⏱late Oct/early Nov) Oxford's Town Hall turns beertopia for a weekend, filled with tank-ards of beer and cider.

Traditional Cotswolds Sports

Despite official disapproval, the ancient and dangerous art of **cheese-rolling** (www.cheese-rolling.co.uk) can be admired on the final Monday of May, when crowds run, tumble and slide down Cooper's Hill, north-east of Painswick, pursuing an 8lb round of Double Gloucester cheese. The prize? The cheese itself – and the glory of catching it.

In late May or early June, in Chipping Campden, the extraordinary **Cotswold Olimpicks** (www.olimpickgames.co.uk), first celebrated in 1612, features the medieval sport of shin kicking, among other events.

Shopping

SHUANG LI / SHUTTERSTOCK ©

Oxford's finest shopping is in the city centre, with independent outlets along the main streets and the national chains in the huge Westgate Shopping Centre. Shops selling locally themed gifts and souvenirs line Broad St and High St in particular. Not far north, Jericho's Walton St holds a handful of boutiques and bookshops.

Cotswolds Food Shopping

Organic, ethically sourced produce has long been a staple in the Cotswolds, and food-lovers will make tempting discoveries in markets, delis and independent food shops all over the region.

Many Cotswolds towns hold farmers markets, where local producers sell seasonal delights. The best of the lot takes place in Stroud every Saturday morning. Check locally, or see the online schedule at www.cotswolds.org.

Best Cotswolds Goodies

Simon Weaver Organic (www.simonweaver.net) Delicious cheese, from a farm near Upper Slaughter.

LoveMyCow (www.lovemycow.com) Organic beef, raised on pastures overlooking Bourton-on-the-Water.

Upton Smokery (www.uptonsmokery.co.uk) Smoked fish and meats, plus weekend barbecues, outside Burford.

Cotswold Ice Cream Company (www.cotswoldicecream.co.uk) Fantastic ice cream, made and sold on a dairy farm in Chedworth, near Northleach.

Best Oxford Shops

Blackwell's Oxford's much-loved bookshop burrows deep beneath the city centre. (pictured; p59)

Ashmolean Shop The museum store is packed with exquisite gifts and craft items. (p89)

Covered Market This lovely old market is a great source of gifts, gewgaws and grub. (p61)

Westgate Shopping Centre Enormous mall, with major brands, department stores and rooftop restaurants. (p60)

Alice's Shop This tiny medieval shop was never managed by a sheep, whatever Lewis Carroll says. (p61)

Tours

To make the most of a visit to Oxford, hear the stories that lurk behind its high walls and closed doorways, and see details you might otherwise miss, it's well worth joining at least one guided tour. Only a walking tour will do: the city centre is too tight-knit to see from a bus, and you can only explore the colleges on foot.

STANISLAV HALCIN / ALAMY STOCK PHOTO ©

Best Oxford Walking Tours

Oxford Official Walking Tours

(📞01865-686441; www.experienceoxfordshire.org; 15-16 Broad St; adult/child from £14/10; ⏱10.45am & 1pm, extra tours 11am & 2pm during busy periods; 👫) Comprehensive two-hour tours of the city and its colleges, plus themed tours, including one on *Alice in Wonderland* and Harry Potter, another on CS Lewis and JRR Tolkien, and a third on Inspector Morse. Book at the tourist office.

Oxford Walking Tours

(📞07790 734387; www.oxfordwalkingtours.com; Trinity College, Broad St; adult/child £13/6; ⏱11am, noon, 1pm, 2pm, 3pm & 4pm; 👫) Informative 90-minute tours on Oxford and its university, departing from Trinity College. Rates include entry to the Bodleian's Divinity School and some colleges. Also weekly literary tours (2pm Wed, adult/child £15/8); ghost tours (£13/6); and Tolkien tours. During the university year, more expensive tours cover student life (10am Mon, Wed and Sun early Oct to mid-Jun, £90/85).

Bill Spectre's Oxford Ghost Trail

(📞07941 041811; www.ghosttrail.org; Oxford Castle; adult/child £10/7; ⏱6.30pm Fri & Sat; 👫) For an entertaining voyage through Oxford's uncanny underbelly, plus the odd magic trick, take a 1¾-hour tour with Victorian undertaker Bill Spectre. No bookings needed, audience participation more than likely.

Footprints Tours

(📞0207-558 8706; www.footprints-tours.com; 5 Broad St; ⏱11am, 12.30pm & 2pm Sun-Fri, 10am, 11am, 12.30pm, 2pm & 3.30pm Sat, extra tours Jul & Aug; 👫) For a two-hour walking tour on Oxford history, simply turn up at 5 Broad St. It's nominally 'free', but payment is by tips. Book ahead for biking, pub and Harry Potter tours; check schedules online.

Oxford City Walk

(📞07530 951320; www.oxfordcitywalk.co.uk; 2hr tour for up to 10 people £45) Bespoke tours tweaked to interests such as architecture, literature, history, science or music. French, German and Italian tours available.

Art

HERITAGE IMAGES / GETTY IMAGES ©

Oxford is home to some magnificent art, notably in the great collections of the Ashmolean and Christ Church, but also in the chapels and public spaces of other colleges. Further intriguing museums and galleries are scattered through the Cotswolds, along with sites associated with William Morris and the Arts and Crafts movement.

Best Art Galleries

Ashmolean Museum From paintings by van Gogh and Goya (pictured) to drawings by Michelangelo and Hiroshige's woodblock prints. (p78)

Christ Church Picture Gallery Masterpieces from Renaissance Italy, created by the likes of Tintoretto, Filippino Lippi, Michelangelo and Leonardo. (p38)

Modern Art Oxford Free, frequently changing exhibitions of the very best in contemporary art, plus talks and workshops. (p49)

Broadway Museum & Art Gallery Closely connected to the Ashmolean, this museum holds works by Reynolds and Gainsborough, among others. (p117)

New College The college chapel holds Jacob Epstein's 8ft-tall statue of the raised Lazarus, swaddled in bandages. (p46)

New Brewery Arts To watch artists and craftspeople at work, and catch the current exhibition, drop in at this lively space in central Cirencester. (p139)

Best of William Morris

Kelmscott Manor Morris bought this lovely Tudor mansion, close to the Thames, with DG Rossetti, and it's still filled with his personal possessions. (p130)

Broadway Tower Thanks to the solitary summer Morris spent here, this hilltop folly holds displays on the

Arts and Crafts movement. (p117)

Exeter College Exeter's 19th-century French-Gothic chapel displays former student William Morris's tapestry, *The Adoration of the Magi*. (p50)

Oxford Union The Oxford Union's Pre-Raphaelite murals were painted by DG Rossetti, William Morris and Edward Burne-Jones. (p52)

St Edmund Hall The chapel of this medieval Oxford college holds a stained-glass window designed by William Morris and Edward Burne-Jones. (p52)

Bibury Morris called this delightful spot, home to the picturesque cottages of Arlington Row, the most beautiful village in England. (p130)

History

For a thousand years, Oxford has stood at the centre of English history. It even served as Charles I's capital city during the Civil War, while its university has attracted illustrious figures, and remarkable collections, from all over the world. The surrounding countryside, especially in the Cotswolds, holds some remarkable ancient sites.

EXPOSE / SHUTTERSTOCK ©

Best Oxford Historical Sites

Christ Church Cardinal Wolsey's college, home to 13 British prime ministers plus Lewis Carroll, simply oozes history. (pictured; p36)

Uffington White Horse Graceful and eerily modern in style, this chalk figure was etched into the hillside 3000 years ago. (p133)

Blenheim Palace This sumptuous home was the gift to the Duke of Marlborough from a grateful nation; in return, it gave the nation Winston Churchill. (p92)

Bodleian Library The wood-panelle Convocation House has thrice served as the seat of England's Parliament. (p40)

Oxford Castle and Prison Incorporating the thousand-year-old St George's Tower, Oxford's castle was used as a prison until 1996. (p46)

Church of St Margaret of Antioch Henry VIII made the pilgrimage to this village church, praying to be granted a son. (p91)

Best Cotswolds Historical Sites

Sudeley Castle Winchcombe's superb castle has an amazing royal history; four Tudor queens walked in its rose garden. (p122)

Chedworth Roman Villa New discoveries are still being unearthed at this dramatic ancient home near Northleach. (p129)

Cold War Experience In a claustrophobic bunker, counter-intuitively dug into a hilltop near Broadway, monitors watched for nuclear attack until 1991. (p119)

Rollright Stones These ancient stones, in a field outside Chipping Norton, originally encircled a Neolithic ceremonial site. (p101)

Minster Lovell Hall Richard III stayed in this long-abandoned manor house; its owner fought alongside him at the 1485 Battle of Bosworth. (p131)

St John the Baptist's Church Burford's magnificent medieval church holds some extraordinary tombs, and served as a prison for dissident Levellers during the Civil War. (p127)

Museums

Thanks to the presence of one of the world's greatest universities, Oxford holds a superb cluster of museums. The Ashmolean especially is outstanding, global in its reach while remaining scrupulously attentive to its Oxford environs. Exploring the Cotswolds, you'll encounter any number of fascinating local museums and galleries.

PATCHAMOL JENSATIENWONG / SHUTTERSTOCK ©

Best Oxford Museums

Ashmolean Museum Truly one of the country's great museums, offering an extraordinary journey through world art, history and archaeology, as well as some absolute-one-of-a-kind treasures. (p78)

Pitt Rivers Museum Follow in the wake of Captain Cook, Victorian explorers and pioneering anthropologists, and discover marvels of human invention and ingenuity. (p80)

Oxford University Museum of Natural History Inspect the mighty teeth of a dinosaur, mourn a murdered dodo that appeared in Alice in Wonderland, or take a selfie with a stuffed bear. (p84)

Museum of the History of Science Housed in the Ashmolean's grand original home, and home to all sorts of scientific artefacts, from Einstein's blackboard to Marconi's radio. (pictured; p48)

Story Museum An exuberant celebration of children's literature, centring on Oxford's own amazing heritage and offering a lively programme of events and activities. (p48)

Best Cotswolds Museums

Corinium Museum As Corinium, Cirencester was one of Roman Britain's most important cities – a story beautifully illustrated by this dazzling modern museum. (p137)

Broadway Museum Courtesy of its close association with Oxford's Ashmolean, Broadway's village museum showcases changing, top-quality displays of artistic and historical treasures. (p117)

Mechanical Music Museum Savour the intriguing sounds of bygone years, amid pre-gramophone gadgets, in this eccentric Northleach museum. (p129)

Court Barn Museum Locally produced handicrafts honour Chipping Campden's crucial 20th-century role in the Arts and Crafts movement. (p110)

Tolsey Museum Disarmingly local in focus, Burford's town museum explores its busy past with gusto. (p127)

Literary Links

As befits such a venerable university town, Oxford is resonant with literary connections. The city's authors are renowned for spinning wondrous tales of fantasy, but plenty of classic books have also described the realities of Oxford life. The Cotswolds too have proved fertile ground for writers.

ALICIA G. MONEDERO / SHUTTERSTOCK ©

Best Oxford Books

An Instance of the Fingerpost *Iain Pears* Multiple-viewpoint mystery set in 17th-century Oxford.

Brideshead Revisited *Evelyn Waugh* A rose-tinged view of pre-war student life.

Alice's Adventures in Wonderland *Lewis Carroll* Alice's Oxford remains present everywhere you look.

Jude the Obscure *Thomas Hardy* The devastating saga of a working-class student in thinly-veiled Christminster.

All Souls *Javier Marias* The travails of a Spanish academic in Oxford.

The Northern Lights *Philip Pullman* Local-born heroine Lyra sees another side of Oxford.

The Moving Toyshop *Edmund Crispin* Absurd comedy thriller from 1946.

To Say Nothing of the Dog *Connie Willis* Time-travel romp set in Victorian Oxford.

Gaudy Night *Dorothy L Sayers* The Oxford-educated Sayers sets a puzzle in the city she loved.

Last Bus to Woodstock *Colin Dexter* The debut of Inspector Morse sets the tone for future adventures.

Best Literary Sites & Events

Bodleian Library The beautiful Bodleian is Oxford's spiritual core. (p40)

Blackwell's Browse for blissful hours in Oxford's favourite bookshop. (p59)

Oxford Literary Festival A 10-day treat for book-lovers, with talks and tours. (p20)

Lamb & Flag Venerable pub, frequented by JRR Tolkien and CS Lewis. (p87)

Weston Library The Weston's free gallery displays literary treasures from the Bodleian. (p47)

Chipping Norton Literary Festival The chief annual get-together for Cotswolds bibliophiles. (p21)

Woolpack Inn Raise a glass to *Cider with Rosie* author Laurie Lee in his local pub in Slad. (p141)

Merton College JRR Tolkien wrote much of *The Lord of the Rings* in Merton's magnificent medieval library. (p47)

Four Perfect Days

Day 1

J.FROO / SHUTTERSTOCK ©

Kickstart explorations of Oxford by touring the **Bodleian Library** (pictured; p40), then visit **Oxford Castle and Prison** (p46), climbing 1000-year-old St George's Tower.

Lunch outside **Vaults & Garden** (p53), admiring the glorious **Radcliffe Camera** (p42), then head to **Christ Church** (p36), Oxford's definitive college, with its stately Great Hall, Cathedral and Picture Gallery. Next stroll through its lush meadow for a pint at the **Head of the River** (p56).

Savour modern British food at **Turl Street Kitchen** (p53), Now it's time to get acquainted with Oxford's legendary pubs, starting in the rambling **Turf Tavern** (p56) before moving on to the **Lamb & Flag** (p87).

Day 2

ASHLEY COOPER / GETTY IMAGES ©

Even in an entire morning in Oxford's **Ashmolean Museum** (p78), you won't see everything. Just follow your heart, through a wonderland of Etruscan statues, Minoan frescoes and Renaissance paintings.

After lunch in the **Ashmolean Rooftop Restaurant** (p86), check out the dodo and dinosaurs in the **Museum of Natural History** (pictured; p84), before heading into the **Pitt Rivers Museum** (p80), an enchanted world of masks and monkey skulls. Continue on to **Magdalen College** (p66), and perhaps rent a punt.

Now cross Magdalen Bridge into southeast Oxford for great Caribbean dishes in **Spiced Roots** (p70) or gastro-pub classics in the **Magdalen Arms** (p71).

Day 3

JUDY DEAN / JUDYPDEAN / 500PX ©

Head for the Cotswolds, via **Blenheim Palace** (pictured; p92), 8 miles northwest of Oxford. Tour its opulent interior and displays on Sir Winston Churchill, then walk through its landscaped gardens. For lunch, drop into Woodstock, where the **King's Arms** (p93) has something to suit all palates.

Continuing northwest, stop at charming **Stow-on-the-Wold** (p104). Wander its central square, then head on to **Broadway** (p116), pausing at **Broadway Tower** (p117), William Morris' hilltop holiday home, before visiting the excellent village **museum** (p117).

Watch the sunset in **Chipping Campden**, swooning at its glowing, honey-hued architecture, then settle in for dinner in the **Eight Bells** (p111).

Day 4

DAVID HUGHES / SHUTTERSTOCK ©

Start another Cotswolds day at grand **Sudeley Castle** (pictured; p122), outside Winchcombe. No fewer than four Tudor queens promenaded through its rose garden.

Then head southwest to delightful **Painswick** (p141) to walk the meandering village lanes and have lunch in the **Falcon** (p141). Depending on the weather, either explore Painswick's superb **Rococo Garden** (p141), or head southeast to celebrates **Cirencester**'s illustrious Roman past in the **Corinium Museum** (p137).

Spend the evening in beautifully preserved **Burford** (p126), northwest, where the golden buildings hold enticing shops, pubs and restaurants. Dine in the **Angel** (p127), ideally out in the garden.

Need to Know

For detailed information, see Survival Guide (p145).

Population
161,300

Language
English

Currency
pound (£)

Visas
Not required for
Australian, Canadian,
New Zealand and US
visitors, and many
other nations, for stays
of up to six months.

Money
ATMs can be found
throughout the city,
and credit cards are
widely accepted.

Time
Greenwich Mean Time
(UTC/GMT)

Mobile phones
The UK uses the GSM
900/1800 network,
which covers the rest of
Europe, Australia and
New Zealand, but isn't
compatible with the
North American GSM
1900. Most modern
mobiles function on
both.

Daily Budget

Budget: Less than £70
Dorm bed: £17.50–28
Cafe, deli or street-food meal: £5–13
Pint of real ale: £3.50
Entry to Ashmolean, Pitt Rivers and other museums: free

Midrange: £70–150
Double room in B&B: £75–130
Main course in midrange restaurant: £12–18
Tickets for major sights (Christ Church, Bodleian Library):
£6–14
Short-hop taxi fares: from £6

Top end: More than £150
Double room in boutique B&B or upmarket hotel: from £130
Three-course meal in restaurant: £25–45
Punt rental or river cruise £17–21

Advance Planning

Three months before If you're coming in
midsummer, or your visit will coincide with
a festival or university event, book your first-
choice accommodation.

One month before Check schedules and buy
tickets for concerts, talks and events. Book
tables at the best-known restaurants.

One week before Make online reservations for
a Bodleian Library tour, and any other walking
tours. Check the weather forecast if you're
planning outdoor activities.

Arriving in Oxford

Most public transport users arrive at the main train or bus stations, just west and northwest of the centre respectively.

🚉 Oxford Station

To walk into the centre from Oxford's train station, head east along Park End St. Buses X13 and X3 run to High St, while bus 5 runs through the centre, via St Aldate's, to Cowley Rd.

🚉 Oxford Parkway

Some trains from London Marylebone run to Oxford Parkway station, 4 miles north of the centre.

🚉 Oxford Bus Station

Oxford's open-air bus station, on Gloucester Green northwest of the centre, is a short walk from all central destinations.

Getting Around

Oxford is a small city, so most visitors walk everywhere. It takes around 10 to 15 minutes to cross the centre on foot.

🚌 Bus

Oxford Bus Company (📞01865-785400; www.oxfordbus.co.uk) and **Stagecoach** (📞01865-772250; www.stagecoachbus.com) serve an extensive network, designed to meet the needs of residents and commuters rather than visitors.

🚲 Bicycle

Cycling is a popular way to get around Oxford for students and visitors alike.

🚕 Taxi

There are taxi ranks at the train and bus stations.

Oxford Neighbourhoods

Jericho & the Science Area (p77)
Jericho is home to the unmissable Ashmolean Museum, while the Science Area holds many of the university's departments.

Cowley Road & Southeast Oxford (p65)
The college is surrounded by meadows and walking paths; nearby are some great drinking places.

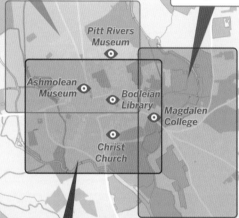

Pitt Rivers Museum

Ashmolean Museum

Bodleian Library

Magdalen College

Christ Church

Central Oxford (p35)
Oxford's main sights are concentrated here. The main core is also filled with cafes, bars, restaurants and shops.

Explore Oxford

With its honey-coloured colleges arrayed in splendour beside the river, the university town of Oxford is a seductive vision of medieval learning and modern charm.

Explore ◈
Central Oxford

Back in the 13th century the majestic medieval buildings that still grace Oxford today were encircled by a fortified wall, within a very compact area. Oxford's main sights are consequently very close to each other indeed – perfect for sightseers. So much of the city's daily life remains focused upon this small core that it's also filled with cafes, bars, restaurants and shops.

Start your day with a tour of the venerable Bodleian Library (p40). Everyone visits its breathtaking Divinity School and sumptuous Duke Humfrey's Library; some also include the glorious Radcliffe Camera (p42). Then admire selected Bodleian treasures in the Weston Library (p47). After lunch outside Vaults & Garden (p53), dip into All Souls (p48) or Merton (p47), then head south to explore Christ Church (p36), and stroll through its riverside meadow. Savour an early-evening pint at the Head of the River (p56) before a modern bistro dinner at Turl Street Kitchen (p53), then while away the evening in more of Oxford's legendary pubs, starting with the rambling Turf Tavern (p56).

Getting There & Around

🏃 Oxford's town centre is less than 10 minutes' walk east from the train station, while its bus station is on its north-western edge, immediately south of Jericho.

🚌 Buses X13 and X3 connect High St with the train station, and head east across Magdalen Bridge. Bus 5 runs between St Aldate's, Westgate Shopping Centre and the train station, and serves Cowley Rd.

Central Oxford Map on p44

Radcliffe Camera (p42) JOE DANIEL PRICE / GETTY IMAGES ©

Top Sights 📷
Christ Church

Thanks to its magnificent buildings, illustrious history and role in the Harry Potter movies, Christ Church is Oxford's most visited college. Established in 1525, it's the university's largest college, if you include its bucolic meadow, and boasts Oxford's grandest quad, as well as its own cathedral and art gallery. Victorian-era don Lewis Carroll immortalised the dean's daughter in Alice in Wonderland.

◉ MAP P44, F4

📞 01865-276492

www.chch.ox.ac.uk

St Aldate's

adult/child Jul & Aug £10/9, Sep-Jun £8/7

🕐 10am-5pm Mon-Sat, from 2pm Sun, last admission 4.15pm

The Great Hall

Self-guided tours of Christ Church head straight from the Meadow Gate entrance to the spectacular Renaissance Great Hall. Surmounted by a hammer-beam roof, it's adorned with portraits of bygone scholars including poet WH Auden, Lewis Carroll, and several British prime ministers. The long-necked female figures on the fireplace inspired a memorable moment in *Alice in Wonderland*.

You may think you've seen the Great Hall before, as Hogwarts' dining hall in the Harry Potter films, but that was a studio-built replica. Professor McGonagall did welcome Harry on the actual fan-vaulted staircase outside, though, in *Harry Potter and the Philosopher's Stone*.

Christ Church Cathedral

Remarkably, Christ Church Cathedral continues to double as both Christ Church's college chapel and Oxford's cathedral. From the 8th century onwards this site held a priory that centred on the Anglo-Saxon shrine of St Frideswide, Oxford's patron saint, and was a major destination for pilgrims.

What's now the cathedral started out as the priory church in the 12th century, and became the chapel of what Cardinal Wolsey founded as Cardinal College in 1525. During the Reformation, St Frideswide's original shrine was destroyed, but Henry VIII made this church a cathedral when he renamed Christ Church in 1546.

The brawny Norman columns inside are topped by elegant vaulting. Check out the stained-glass windows, which as well as a 1320 rendition of the murder of Thomas Becket include an 1878 portrait of St Catherine by former Oxford student Edward Burne-Jones. He modelled the saint on Edith Liddell, daughter of the dean and sister of Alice, who had died two years previously, and is buried outside.

★ **Top Tips**

o Always say 'Christ Church', not 'Christ Church College'.

o Arrive early to avoid queues.

o The Great Hall frequently closes to visitors at lunchtime (noon–2pm).

o There's no charge to visit the Cathedral for prayer or services.

o Access to Christ Church Meadow is free, from dawn to dusk.

o Free tours explore the Picture Gallery at 2.30pm on Monday.

✖ **Take a Break**

Follow the Thames southwest from the meadow to reach the lovely Head of the River (p56) pub.

Head northeast from the meadow into the riverside Botanic Garden (p69) for coffee and a snack.

The 15th-century **cloister** originally formed part of the Priory of St Frideswide.

Tom Tower

The stately 17th-century Tom Tower, its topmost portion designed by former student Sir Christopher Wren, dominates Tom Quad. Tom Gate, the official college entrance below, is not open to mere tourists. **Great Tom**, the tower's 6-tonne bell, chimes 101 times at 9.05pm nightly – Oxford is five minutes west of Greenwich – to sound the curfew imposed on the original students.

Tom Quad

Tom Quad is Oxford's definitive college quadrangle, with the elegant figure of Mercury poised above its central pond. Lewis Carroll had rooms on the northwest corner, while Alice Liddell lived in the deanery opposite. Carroll joked that it was 'vulgar' to abbreviate Tom Quad: 'You should always be polite, even when speaking to a Quadrangle'.

Christ Church Picture Gallery

Long one of Oxford's wealthiest colleges, Christ Church has amassed an exceptional art collection. Dating largely from the 14th to the 18th centuries, it's displayed in a small modern gallery that was tucked in behind the cathedral during the 1960s. Italian Renaissance masterpieces include Filippino Lippi's *The Wounded Centaur* and Tintoretto's *Martyrdom of St Lawrence*, while a selection of drawings by the likes of

Christ Church from Christ Church Meadow

An Oxford Puzzle: Lewis Carroll & Alice Liddell

On a sunny summer's day in Oxford, long ago – 4 July 1862, to be precise – Christ Church mathematics don Charles Dodgson (1832–98) took the three daughters of the dean, Edith, Alice and Ina Liddell, out rowing on the Thames. En route, he spun the story that he subsequently published under the pen-name of Lewis Carroll. Both *Alice's Adventures in Wonderland* and its sequel, *Through The Looking-Glass*, became classics of children's literature.

Besides bursting with puzzles, parodies and conundrums, both books abound in references to Oxford people and places. Dodgson himself was the Dodo; thanks to a slight stutter he'd often introduce himself as 'Do-do-Dodgson'. Rev Robinson Duckworth, his rowing companion that 'golden afternoon', was the Duck, while locals also recognised the originals of the Mad Hatter and other characters. A little grocery store opposite Christ Church became the sheep's shop, while the Treacle Well can still be seen in nearby Binsey.

There is, of course, a less charming side to this familiar tale. Long before *Alice's Adventures in Wonderland* appeared in print, Dodgson had become estranged from the Liddell family. After a boat trip with the girls on 25 June 1863, he reported in his diary 'a pleasant expedition with a very pleasant conclusion'. The next few diary entries are missing, but Mrs Liddell, appalled by some unknown event, forbade further contact, and he almost never saw the girls again. Some suggest he proposed marriage either to Alice, then aged 11, or to her sister Lorina, then 14.

Dodgson once declared 'I am fond of children, except boys'. It's often argued that his interest in young girls, and hobby of photographing them naked, were not unusual for the era, when such girls were seen as symbolising innocence. On the other hand, he stopped doing so because Oxford mothers denied him access to their daughters. Almost none of those images now survive; he destroyed them shortly before his death.

Michelangelo, Leonardo da Vinci and Dürer is always on show. Admission is half-price with a Christ Church ticket.

Christ Church Meadow

A lush expanse that extends south to the Thames and east to the Cherwell, the verdant wedge of Christ Church Meadow is defined by the confluence of the two rivers. Its spacious avenues and riverside paths are ideal for a leisurely half-hour walk, though its central swathe is fenced off to hold the college's resident herd of longhorn cattle.

Top Sights 📷
Bodleian Library

At least five kings, dozens of prime ministers and Nobel laureates, and luminaries such as Oscar Wilde, CS Lewis and JRR Tolkien have studied in Oxford's Bodleian Library, a magnificent survivor from the Middle Ages. Take in its overall splendour for free from the central quad; pay £1 to see its 15th-century Divinity School; or explore the entire ensemble on a guided tour.

◎ MAP P44, B5

📞 01865-287400

www.bodleian.ox.ac.uk/ bodley; Catte St;

Divinity School £1, with audio tour £3.50, guided tours £6-14

🕙 9am-5pm Mon-Sat, from 11am Sun

Divinity School

All Bodleian tours, including the two most popular daily options – the 'mini-tour' (30 minutes, £6) and the 'standard tour' (one hour, £8) – start in its exquisite medieval Divinity School. A masterpiece of English Gothic architecture, this was founded around 1423, as the first purpose-built teaching room of Oxford University. Divinity was then regarded as the 'Queen of the Sciences', and students were subjected to oral examinations here in Latin and Greek. Take a close look at its superb fan-vaulted ceiling, and along with three 'Green Men' – a familiar folk motif – you'll spot the initials of benefactors including Thomas Kemp, who features 84 times, plus those of craftsmen who worked on it. In the Harry Potter films, the Divinity School served as Hogwarts' infirmary.

Convocation House

The grand wood-panelled chamber known as Convocation House, beyond the Divinity School and included on standard Bodleian tours, was the original meeting place of the university's ruling body. It briefly served as the seat of the English Parliament three times, once under Charles I (during the Civil War) and twice under Charles II, when it became a refuge from the Great Plague. Nelson Mandela was awarded an honorary degree here in 1997.

Duke Humfrey's Library

Duke Humfrey's Library, the Bodleian's original core, is upstairs, above the Divinity School. Completed in 1488, it's named after the youngest brother of Henry V of Agincourt fame, an avid bibliophile who features in a couple of Shakespeare's plays. Humfrey donated the initial collection, including classical translations he'd commissioned himself.

You can't enter this magnificently decorated medieval room, let alone inspect the ancient

★ Top Tips

o The only areas included on all Bodleian tours are the Divinity School and Duke Humfrey's Library.

o Only two weekly tours visit Radcliffe Camera; if you want to see it, plan ahead and book early.

o Be sure to visit the free Weston Library nearby, which exhibits choice historical highlights from the Bodleian's collection.

✕ Take a Break

At Vaults & Garden (p53), on the southern side of Radcliffe Sq, you can, as the name suggests, pick up a meal in the church vaults, then sit outside in full view of Radcliffe Camera.

One of Oxford's most enchanting old pubs, the Turf Tavern (p56), lies a short walk east of the library; turn left at the Bridge of Sighs.

tomes chained to its shelves, but every tour allows you to peer into it from the 17th-century extension at one end. Amazingly, no artificial lighting was permitted in the library – not even candles – until 1929.

Portraits of the founders of Oxford's original colleges line its walls. One lone woman stands out – Lady Dervorguilla (1210–90), from Galloway in Scotland, who was the widow of John Balliol and saw through the completion of his namesake college after his death.

In the Harry Potter films, this was the Hogwarts library.

Radcliffe Camera

Surely Oxford's most photographed landmark, the circular, sandy-gold **Radcliffe Camera**

(📞01865-287400; www.bodleian.ox.ac. uk; Radcliffe Sq; tours £14; ⏰Bodleian tours 9.15am Wed & Sat, 11.15am & 1.15pm Sun) stands proud at the centre of Radcliffe Sq. Built in grand Palladian style between 1737 and 1749, financed by a legacy from Oxford physician Dr John Radcliffe and topped by Britain's third-largest dome, this was originally the 'Radcliffe Library'. It's only been a 'camera', which simply means 'room', since 1860, when it became what it remains, a reading room of the Bodleian Library.

Visitors can only see its beautiful interior, columned and flooded with light, as part of an extended 1½-hour tour. These access the Camera via an underground passageway known as the Gladstone Link.

Interior of dome, Radcliffe Camera

The Story of the Bodleian

When Duke Humfrey died in 1447, he left 281 precious manuscripts to Oxford University, prompting the construction of the superb library that bore his name. A century later, however, during the Reformation, the library's entire collection was destroyed and dispersed, seen by the new Protestant authorities as tainted with pernicious Catholic doctrines.

The university thus lacked a library until 1598, when Sir Thomas Bodley, a fellow of Merton College, came to the rescue. Retiring to Oxford after a diplomatic career, Bodley dedicated himself to refurbishing and re-establishing what therefore became the Bodleian Library in 1602. His daring modern ideas included not chaining each individual book, but keeping them on secure high-level galleries to which access could be constantly monitored, an innovation he'd seen in the library of Philip II of Spain.

In 1610 Bodley made a crucial agreement with the Stationers' Company of London, entitling his library to receive a copy of every single book published in the UK. That made it the first of what are now six such 'legal deposit' libraries in the UK and Ireland. Having started with just 20 books, the Bodleian currently holds more than 12 million items, contains 117 miles of shelving and has seating space for up to 2500 readers. Several thousand new books and articles continue to arrive every Wednesday, all needing to be catalogued and stored.

The Bodleian has never been a lending library. No one, not even Charles I when he ruled from Oxford during the Civil War, has ever been allowed to borrow a book. All readers have instead to be physically present, and, to this day, all have to swear Bodley's Oath, vowing not to bring fire or flames into the library.

Old Schools Quadrangle

The Bodleian's oldest buildings surround a Jacobean Gothic courtyard known as the Old Schools Quadrangle, to which access is free. The quad is dominated on its eastern side by the Tower of the Five Orders, an ornate structure whose columns illustrate the five classical orders of architecture – from the bottom up, Tuscan, Doric, Ionic, Corinthian and Composite.

Chancellor's Court

The brooding dark Chancellor's Court, beyond Convocation House, was the seat of legal authority within the university. Both Oscar Wilde and Romantic poet Percy Bysshe Shelley went on trial here, for debt and promoting atheism respectively.

Central Oxford

A **B** **C** **D**

1

Cardigan St
Great Clarendon St
Wellington St
Walton Cres
Richmond Rd
Walton La
Worcester Pl
Little Clarendon St
Lamb & Flag Passage
Pusey St
St Cross College
St John St
St Giles
Ashmolean Museum
Magdalen St East
Magdalen St

2

Oxford Canal
Worcester St
Worcester College
Beaumont St
44
✕29
St Cormarket
36
41
George St
28
25
40
St Michael's St
39
Oxford Union
19
45

3

Oxford Train Station
Rewley Rd
Hythe Bridge St
Fisher Row
Walton St
Gloucester Green
Bus Station
Nuffield College
George St Mews
New Inn Hall St

Botley Rd
Park End St
Tidmarsh La
New Rd
1 Oxford Castle and Prison
Queen St

4

Becket St
Hollybush Row
St Thomas St
Paradise St
Castle St
Old Greyfriars St
Modern Art Oxford
8
St Ebbes St

Enlargement

5

0 ___ 100 m
0 ___ 0.05 miles

34
Holywell St
Bath Pl
Balliol College
18
Trinity College
10
3 Weston Library
11 Bridge of Sighs
32
Broad St
43 46
52
15 Sheldonian Theatre
7
Bodleian Library
2 New College

i
51
24 ✕
Museum of the History of Science

Ship St
Jesus College
Exeter College
12
Brasenose La
Radcliffe Camera
Catte St
47

6

Market St
49
22
42
Covered Market
Brasenose College
9
St Mary's Passage
Radcliffe Sq
17 ✕
13
University Church of St Mary the Virgin
All Souls College
5

River Thames

A **B** **C** **D**

Map labels

- Museum Rd
- Parks Rd
- South Parks Rd
- Mansfield College
- Mansfield Rd
- Manor Rd
- Wadham College
- Manchester College
- Jowett Walk
- St Cross Rd
- Longwall St
- Grove Deer Park
- See Enlargement
- Holywell St
- ✕ 21
- Broad St
- Ship St
- Catte St
- Queen's La
- Magdalen College
- Market St
- Turl St
- Brasenose La
- St Mary's Passage
- ◉ Queen's College
- ◉ 14
- 20 St Edmund Hall
- ✕ 30
- High St
- Addison's Walk
- 37 🍴
- ✕ 31
- University College
- Magpie La
- Logic La
- 27
- 48 🛍
- ◉ 16 Cartax Tower
- 26 ✕
- 38
- Alfred St
- St Aldate's
- 35
- Oriel St
- 27
- Merton St
- Rose La
- Magdalen Bridge
- 🛍 Story Museum
- ◉ 6 Pembroke St
- Blue Boar St
- Oriel Sq
- ◉ Merton College 4
- Dead Man's Walk
- Botanic Garden
- Christ Church College
- Christ Church ◉
- Merton Gve
- Merton Field
- Brewer St
- Rose Pl
- 50 🛍
- Speedwell St
- Broad Walk
- River Cherwell
- Thames St
- Christ Church Meadow
- Poplar Walk
- 🍴 33
- Folly Bridge
- Salter Bros

For reviews see

◉	Top Sights	p36
◉	Sights	p46
✕	Eating	p52
🍴	Drinking	p56
★	Entertainment	p59
🛍	Shopping	p59

0 — 400 m
0 — 0.2 miles

Sights

Oxford Castle and Prison

CASTLE

1 MAP P44, C4

Little now remains of Oxford Castle, which was built for William the Conqueror in 1071, and largely destroyed after the English Civil War because the defeated Royalists had used it as a prison. Entertaining theatrical tours, though, led by costumed guides and departing every 20 minutes in peak season, now lead through the parts that survive – including prison cells which quite unbelievably remained in use until 1996 – and provide an enjoyable overview of Oxford's extraordinary history. (☏01865-260666; www.oxfordcastleandprison.co.uk; 44-46 Oxford Castle; adult/child £11.50/7.95; ⌚tours 10am-4.20pm)

New College

COLLEGE

2 MAP P44, C5

New College isn't really *that* new. Established in 1379 as Oxford's first undergraduate college, it's a glorious Perpendicular Gothic ensemble. Treasures in the chapel include superb medieval stained glass and Sir Jacob Epstein's disturbing 1951 statue of Lazarus, wrapped in his shroud; in term time, visitors can attend the beautiful choral Evensong service (6.15pm nightly). The 15th-century

Oxford, Capital of England

During the English Civil War, Oxford unexpectedly became the capital of (Royalist) England. The first major battle of the war, pitting King Charles I and his 'Cavaliers' against the Parliament-supporting 'Roundheads', was fought in October 1642, at Edgehill, 30 miles north. Both sides claimed victory, but Charles found that his way back to London was blocked, and came to Oxford instead.

It remained his capital for the next four years. Most students left, freeing up accommodation for Charles' army, but university life went on. Two of his sons, future kings Charles II and James II, were awarded degrees.

The King made his home in Christ Church, while Queen Henrietta lived in Merton College; a passageway was opened up between the two. Meanwhile, makeshift fortifications were erected around the city, and artillery installed.

As the end approached, in April 1646, the King fled Oxford for the last time, disguised as a manservant. It was his nephew Prince Rupert, the commander of Royal cavalry, who finally surrendered to the Parliamentarian forces, known as the New Model Army, at Christ Church on 20 June 1646.

cloisters and evergreen oak featured in *Harry Potter and the Goblet of Fire*, while the dining hall is the oldest in Oxbridge. (📞01865-279500; www.new.ox.ac.uk; Holywell St; adult/child £5/4; 🕐11am-5pm Easter-Oct, 2-4pm Nov-Feb)

Weston Library LIBRARY

3 ◉ MAP P44, B5

Opened as the New Bodleian Library by King George VI in 1946, and renamed following a modernist overhaul in 2015, the Weston Library remains an extension of the Bodleian across the road, with almost 25 miles of shelving in its basement alone. Its two free galleries display selected 'Treasures from the Bodleian', ranging from manuscripts by the likes of Mary Shelley or JRR Tolkien to the original Magna Carta. There's also a light-filled cafe. (📞01865-287400; www.bodleian.ox.ac.uk/weston; Broad St; admission free; 🕐10am-5pm Mon-Sat, from 11am Sun)

Merton College COLLEGE

4 ◉ MAP P44, F4

Founded in 1264, peaceful and elegant Merton is one of Oxford's three original colleges. Like the other two, Balliol and University, it considers itself the oldest, arguing that it was the first to adopt collegiate planning, bringing scholars and tutors together into a formal community and providing them with a planned residence. Its distinguishing architectural features include large gargoyles, whose expressions suggest that they're about to throw up, and the

Merton College

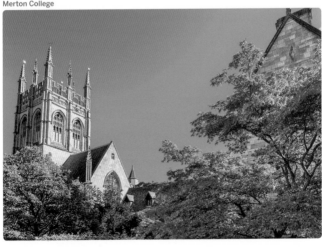

Visiting the Colleges

Not all colleges open to visitors, and none lets visitors penetrate all that deeply into its mysteries, only allowing access to areas such as dining halls, chapels and one or two 'quads' (quadrangles). A select few – like Christ Church, with its dramatic Great Hall – genuinely count as tourist attractions. Otherwise, though, the chief pleasure of visiting an Oxford college is the sense of getting a glimpse behind the scenes, into a rarefied world of scholarship and privilege.

charming, diminutive 14th-century Mob Quad – the first college quad. (01865-276310; www.merton.ox.ac.uk; Merton St; adult/child £3/free; 2-5pm Mon-Fri, from 10am Sat & Sun)

All Souls College COLLEGE

5 MAP P44, C6

One of Oxford's wealthiest and most tranquil colleges, All Souls was founded as a centre of prayer and learning in 1438. Much of its facade dates from that era, while the smaller Front Quad has remained largely unchanged for five centuries. The eye-catching mock-Gothic towers on the North Quad, though, were the work of Nicholas Hawksmoor in 1710, and were originally lambasted for ruining Oxford's skyline. The North

Quad also contains a beautiful 17th-century sundial designed by Christopher Wren. (01865-279379; www.asc.ox.ac.uk; High St; admission free; 2-4pm Sun-Fri, closed Aug)

Story Museum MUSEUM

6 MAP P44, E4

Conceived in celebration of Oxford's unparalleled storytelling heritage, the Story Museum sprawls its way through a courtyard complex that includes various rooms honouring the likes of Lewis Carroll, Phillip Pullman and Wallace and Gromit. Visitors can simply walk through, treating it as a museum, but its real purpose is a performance space, hosting an ever-changing program of storytelling sessions and live shows. Check the website for details. There's also an on-site cafe. (01865-807600; www.storymuseum.org.uk; 42 Pembroke St; day tickets adult/child £7.50/5, event prices vary; museum 10am-5pm Mon-Sat, 11am-4pm Sun in school holidays, 10am-5pm Fri & Sat, 11am-4pm Sun rest of year;)

Museum of the History of Science MUSEUM

7 MAP P44, B5

Students of science will swoon at this fascinating museum, stuffed to the ceilings with awesome astrolabes, astonishing orreries and early electrical apparatus. Housed in the lovely 17th-century building that held the original Ashmolean Museum, it displays everything from cameras that belonged to Lewis Carroll and Lawrence of Arabia to a wireless receiver used by Marconi in 1896 and a blackboard that was covered with equations by Einstein in 1931, when he was invited to give three lectures on relativity. (☎01865-277293; www.mhs.ox.ac.uk; Broad St; admission free; ⏰noon-5pm Tue-Sun)

Modern Art Oxford MUSEUM

8 ◉ MAP P44, D4

Showcasing stimulating temporary exhibitions in its bright, white, airy galleries, and graced with a spacious cafe and a good shop, this excellent museum is well worth anyone's time. Check out the program of upcoming talks and workshops; there's always something interesting going on. (☎01865-722733; www.modernartoxford.org.uk; 30 Pembroke St; admission free; ⏰10am-5pm Tue-Sat, noon-5pm Sun; ♿)

Brasenose College COLLEGE

9 ◉ MAP P44, B6

Small, select and elegant, Brasenose College was founded in 1509. A Brasenose Hall, belonging to Oxford University, already stood here by 1262, however, and when rebellious students relocated to Stamford, Lincolnshire, in 1333, they took its 'brass nose', or brazen door-knocker, with them. In 1890, therefore, the college bought what had become a girls' school in Stamford, seized the knocker from its front door, and fixed it for

evermore above the high table in the dining hall. (☎01865-277830; www.bnc.ox.ac.uk; Radcliffe Sq; £2; ⏰10-11.30am & 2-5pm Mon-Fri, 9.30-10.30am & 2-5pm Sat & Sun)

Trinity College COLLEGE

10 ◉ MAP P44, A5

Founded in 1555, this small college boasts a lovely 17th-century garden quad, designed by Sir Christopher Wren. Its exquisite chapel, a masterpiece of English baroque, contains a limewood altar screen adorned with flowers and fruit carved by master craftsman Grinling Gibbons in 1694, and is looking fabulous after recent restoration work. Famous students have included Cardinal Newman, William Pitt the Elder, two other

Academic Attire

Don't be surprised to see students wandering around Oxford in black gowns, black 'mortarboard' caps, white bow ties and (for graduates) colourful hoods. This is the official academic dress known as sub fusc, from the Latin sub fuscus, meaning dark brown (yes, even though it's actually black). Oxford students are required to wear it when they take their exams and when they collect their degrees, while some colleges require it every night when dining in the hall.

British prime ministers, and the fictional Jay Gatsby, the Great Gatsby himself. (📞01865-279900; www.trinity.ox.ac.uk; Broad St; adult/child £3/2; ⏰9.30am-noon & 2pm-dusk)

Bridge of Sighs BRIDGE

11 ◉ MAP P44, B5

As you stroll along New College Lane, look up at the steeped Bridge of Sighs linking the two halves of Hertford College. Completed in 1914, it's sometimes erroneously referred to as a copy of the famous bridge in Venice, but it looks much more like that city's Rialto Bridge. (Hertford Bridge; New College Lane)

Exeter College COLLEGE

12 ◉ MAP P44, A6

Founded in 1314, Exeter is known for its elaborate 17th-century dining hall, which celebrated its 400th birthday in 2018, and ornate Victorian Gothic chapel, a psychedelic blast of gold mosaic and stained glass that holds a tapestry created by former students William Morris and Edward Burne Jones,*The Adoration of the Magi*. Exeter also inspired former student Philip Pullman to create fictional Jordan College in *His Dark Materials*. (📞01865-279600; www.exeter.ox.ac.uk; Turl St; admission free; ⏰2-5pm)

University Church of St Mary the Virgin CHURCH

13 ◉ MAP P44, B6

The ornate 14th-century spire of Oxford's university church is arguably the dreamiest of the city's legendary 'dreaming spires'. Otherwise, this is famous as the site where three Anglican bishops, including the first Protestant archbishop of Canterbury, Thomas Cranmer, were tried for heresy in 1556, during the reign of Mary I. All three were later burned at the stake on Broad St. Visitors can climb the church's 1280 tower (£4) for excellent views of the adjacent Radcliffe Camera. (📞01865-279111; www.university-church.ox.ac.uk; High St; church free, tower £4; ⏰9am-5pm Mon-Sat, from noon Sun Sep-Jun, 9am-6pm daily Jul & Aug)

Queen's College COLLEGE

14 ◉ MAP P44, G3

Known for its musical excellence, this college is steeped in esteem and heritage. Although founded in 1341, its main claims to architectural fame are the wonderful examples of neoclassical architecture from the 17th and 18th centuries. Enter from High St, and you're met by the large green quad surrounded by uniform stone arches. If you get a chance, watch the college choir perform on site. (📞01865-279120; www.queens.ox.ac.uk; High St; ⏰by prior arrangement only)

Sheldonian Theatre

THEATRE

15 MAP P44, B5

Built from 1663 onwards to provide an appropriately grand setting for the university's degree ceremonies – a function it still performs – this monumental building was the first major work of Sir Christopher Wren, then a professor of astronomy. Modelled on Rome's classical Theatre of Marcellus, it's rectangular at the front and semicircular behind. The remarkably long ceiling of its main hall, held up by ingenious braces made of shorter timbers, bears 17th-century murals depicting the triumph of truth over ignorance. (☏01865-277299; www.admin.ox.ac.uk/sheldonian; Broad St; adult/child £3.50/2.50; ⏱10am-1pm & 2-4.30pm Mon-Sat Feb-Oct, to 3pm Nov-Jan)

Carfax Tower

TOWER

16 MAP P44, E4

All that remains of St Martin's Church, demolished in 1896, this 13th-century landmark looms over what has been a crossroads for 1000 years. Climb the 99 steps of its spiral staircase for good views over the city centre. (Queen St; adult/child £2.70/1.70; ⏱10am-5pm)

St Mary's Passage

STREET

17 MAP P44, B6

With a doorway sporting a lion's head knocker, flanked by two golden fawns, this tiny alley is often said to have inspired elements of CS Lewis' magical world in *The*

Bridge of Sighs

Chronicles of Narnia. That may or may not be true, but it's certainly a pretty little corner, tucked between High St and the much-photographed Radcliffe Camera.

Balliol College   COLLEGE

18 ⊙ MAP P44, A5

Dating its foundation to 'about' 1263, Balliol College claims to be the oldest college in Oxford, though its current buildings are largely 19th-century. Scorch marks on the huge Gothic wooden doors between its inner and outer quadrangles, however, supposedly date from the public burning of three Protestant bishops, including Archbishop of Canterbury Thomas Cranmer, in 1556. (☎01865-277777; www.balliol.ox.ac.uk; Broad St; adult/child £3/1; ⏰10am-5pm, to dusk in winter)

Oxford Union   LIBRARY

19 ⊙ MAP P44, D3

Famed worldwide as a debating society, and also known for attracting prominent international speakers, Oxford's legendary Union is largely off-limits to non-members. It is however possible to visit its library, home to some marvellous Pre-Raphaelite murals painted between 1857 and 1859 by Dante Gabriel Rossetti, William Morris and Edward Burne-Jones. Depicting scenes from the Arthurian legends, such as Arthur's first victory with the sword Excalibur, they can be tricky to see on bright days, as they surround the flower-shaped windows. (☎01865-241353; www.oxford-union.org; Frewin Ct; £1.50; ⏰9.30am-5pm Mon-Fri)

St Edmund Hall   COLLEGE

20 ⊙ MAP P44, G3

Founded at some point before 1317, St Edmund Hall is the sole survivor of Oxford's original medieval halls, the teaching institutions that preceded the colleges. 'Teddy Hall' to residents, it became a college itself in 1957, and holds a chapel decorated by William Morris and Edward Burne-Jones. Mohawk chief Oronhyatekha studied here in 1862, and eloped with the principal's daughter. (☎01865-279000; www.seh.ox.ac.uk; Queen's Lane; admission free; ⏰10am-4pm)

Eating

Edamamé   JAPANESE £

21 ✕ MAP P44, G2

No wonder a constant stream of students squeeze in and out of this tiny diner – it's Oxford's top spot for delicious, gracefully simple Japanese cuisine. Changing noodle and curry specials include fragrant chicken miso ramen, tofu stir-fries, or mackerel with soba noodles; it only serves sushi or sashimi on Thursday evenings. No bookings; arrive early and be prepared to wait. (☎01865-246916; www.edamame.co.uk; 15 Holywell St; mains £7-10.50; ⏰11.30am-2.30pm Wed, 11.30am-2.30pm & 5-8.30pm Thu-Sat, noon-3.30pm Sun; 🖫)

Covered Market

MARKET £

22 ⊗ MAP P44, A6

A haven for impecunious students, this indoor marketplace holds 20 restaurants, cafes and takeaways. Let anyone loose here, and something's sure to catch their fancy. Brown's no-frills cafe, famous for its apple pies, is the longest-standing veteran. Look out too for Georgina's, serving quiches and burgers upstairs; Burt's superlative Cookies; two excellent pie shops; and good Thai and Chinese options. (www.oxford-coveredmarket. co.uk; Market St; ⊗vary, some close Sun; 🛜🖋👫)

Vaults & Garden

CAFE £

23 ⊗ MAP P44, C6

This beautiful lunch venue spreads from the vaulted 14th-century Old Congregation House of the University Church into a garden facing the Radcliffe Camera. Come early, and queue at the counter to choose from wholesome organic specials such as leek and potato soup, tofu *massaman* curry, or slow-roasted lamb *tajine*. Breakfast and afternoon tea (those scones!) are equally good. (📞01865-279112; www. thevaultsandgarden.com; University Church of St Mary the Virgin, Radcliffe Sq; mains £7-10.50; ⊗9am-6pm; 🛜🖋)

Turl Street Kitchen

MODERN BRITISH ££

24 ⊗ MAP P44, A5

Whatever time you drop into this laid-back, not-quite-scruffy, seductively charming all-day bistro, with its fairy lights and faded-wood tables, you can expect to eat well. Fresh local produce is thrown into creative combinations, with the changing menu featuring the likes of roasted beetroot, braised lamb, or, on Sunday, roast beef and Yorkshire pudding. It also serves good cakes and coffee. (📞01865-264171; www.turlstreetkitchen.co.uk; 16-17 Turl St; mains £10-16; ⊗8-10am, noon-2.30pm & 6.30-10pm; 🖋)

Handle Bar

CAFE £

25 ⊗ MAP P44, D3

Upstairs above a bike shop, this chatty, friendly cafe has bikes galore, including penny-farthings, dangling from its ceiling and white-painted brick walls. A tad more hippy than hipster, it's usually packed with students, professionals and lucky tourists. They're here for luscious, health-focused bites, like spiced avocado-and-feta toast, roasted chicken breast and fresh-fruit smoothie 'pots', plus tasty cakes, teas and coffees. (📞01865-251315; www.handlebaroxford.co.uk; Bike Zone, 28-31 St Michael's St; dishes £8-13; ⊗8am-6pm Mon & Tue, to 11pm Wed-Fri, from 9am Sat, 10am-5pm Sun; 🛜🖋)

Headhunters of the Sheldonian

The pillars that punctuate the exterior railings of the Sheldonian are decorated with 13 mighty sculpted busts. Carved by William Bird in 1669, they were originally commissioned by Sir Christopher Wren, with another four added soon afterwards to adorn what was then the Ashmolean, next door. Each one weighs approximately one ton. No one knows whom they represent, or for that matter why each sports a different style of beard. Although they've had many nicknames over the years, from 'the Philosophers' to 'the 12 Apostles', they've been generally known for the last century or so as the 'Heads of the Emperors'.

As the whole lot had to be replaced in 1868 and 1972, the current lot are actually the third set. Which begs the question, what happened to the old ones? Around 20 woeful weatherbeaten heads have turned up in gardens dotted throughout Oxford, and the university launched an appeal in 2018 to find the remaining seven thought still to exist. Once they're found, they plan to stage a grand reunion of discarded emperors in the Weston Library.

Chiang Mai Kitchen   THAI ££

26 ✘ MAP P44, E4

Real-deal Thai cuisine in central Oxford, in a fine medieval building tucked down a little alleyway. As well as the expected curries, with plenty of seafood, rice and noodle favourites, it serves standout classics such as stir-fried chicken with cashew nuts and, among excellent vegetarian options, a sensational, tear-jerkingly hot *sôm-ɖam* (spicy papaya salad). (☎01865-202233; www.chiangmaikitchen.co.uk; 130a High St; mains £8.50-17; ☾noon-10.30pm Mon-Sat, to 10pm Sun; ✈)

Grand Café   TEAHOUSE £

27 ✘ MAP P44, G3

Boasting of being England's first-ever coffee house – though not, unlike its rival opposite, open ever since – the Grand looks very much the part, with its columns and gold leaf. While it serves sandwiches, bagels and a towering afternoon tea (from £18), it's the patisserie counter that's the real attraction: fresh, sweet pastry tarts and feather-light *millefeuilles* pair brilliantly with tea. (☎01865-204463; www.thegrandcafe.co.uk; 84 High St; patisserie items £5-7; mains £9-13; ☾9am-6.30pm Mon-Thu, to 7pm Fri-Sun; ♿)

Society Café

CAFE £

28  MAP P44, D3

Stripped-down, dazzling-white cafe, with a scattering of light-wood Scandi-style tables, where you can enjoy a good cup of coffee in a relaxed ambience. The highly trained baristas are passionate about hot drinks, so you always get something great, while the cakes are delicious and fresh, and the chai spicy. Vegan options available. (☎01225-442433; www.society-cafe.com; 16 St Michael's St; flat white £2.80; ⊙7.30am-6.30pm Mon-Sat, 9.30am-6pm Sun; ☂☝)

Organic Deli Café

CAFE £

29 MAP P44, D2

Only if you're looking for this appetising little wholefood cafe are you likely to wander down the central alleyway where it's hidden. Make the effort, and you're rewarded with good cooked breakfasts, filling sandwiches and some hearty old-fashioned baked goods, like Grandad's (gluten-free) Fruit Cake. Alternatively, don't bother getting out of bed – it delivers throughout Oxford. (☎01865-364853; www.organicwholefoods.co.uk; 24 Friars Entry, off Gloucester Green; mains £5-10; ⊙8am-6pm; ☎☂)

Queen's Lane Coffee House

CAFE £

30 MAP P44, G3

Proudly claiming to be Europe's oldest continually working coffee house, dating back to the 1650s, this family-run central cafe

Grand Café

MICHAEL WINTERS / ALAMY STOCK PHOTO ©

A Cruise on the River

If you fancy a scenic cruise along the Thames, passing college boathouses and busy riverside pubs, head to **Salter Bros** (Map p44, E6; 01865-243421; www.salterssteamers.co.uk; Folly Bridge; punt/rowboat/motorboat per hour £20/20/45; 10am-6pm Easter-Oct), just south of Christ Church. Their options include the 8-mile, two-hour trip to the historic market town of Abingdon (9.15am and 2.30pm, late May to early September, adult/child £20.80/11.70), and a 2½-hour Alice in Wonderland cruise (£17.50/£10).

preserves many original features. Rather than trading on nostalgia, though, it specialises in supplying students and tourists with reliable, no-nonsense fry-ups, Turkish-style kebabs and mixed plates, and big slices of cake, along with steaming mugs of dark, rich Turkish coffee. (01865-240082; www.qlcoffeehouse.com; 40 High St; lunch £5-9; 7.30am-8pm;)

Quod
MODERN BRITISH ££

31 MAP P44, F3

This smart, conspicuous, central brasserie, set in a former bank, could be anywhere in the world, but there's no faulting its efficient all-day delivery of a tick-all-the-boxes menu that ranges from pizzas and burgers to steaks, roast cod or goat's cheese, leek and celery pie. The two-course set lunch/early dinner menu (noon to 6pm Monday to Friday, £12.95) is the best value. (01865-202505; www.quod.co.uk; Old Bank Hotel, 92-94 High St; mains £11.50-26; 7am-11pm;)

Drinking

Turf Tavern
PUB

32 MAP P44, C5

Squeezed down an alleyway and subdivided into endless nooks and crannies, this medieval rabbit warren dates from around 1381. The definitive Oxford pub, this is where Bill Clinton famously 'did not inhale'; other patrons have included Oscar Wilde, Stephen Hawking and Margaret Thatcher. Home to a fabulous array of real ales and ciders, it's always pretty crowded, but there's outdoor seating, too. (01865-243235; www.turftavern-oxford.co.uk; 4-5 Bath Pl; 11am-11pm;)

Head of the River
PUB

33 MAP P44, E6

For a summer-evening riverside drink, central Oxford holds no finer setting than the Thames-facing terrace of this imposing former warehouse – hence the hand-cranked crane, still outside – and later a boatyard. The beer's good, courtesy of Fullers brewery. There's plenty of room indoors – as well as decent food, and a stylish hotel upstairs – but the lure of the river is irresistible. (📞01865-721600; www.headoftheriveroxford.co.uk; Folly Bridge, St Aldates; ⏱8am-10.30pm Sun-Thu, to 11.30pm Fri & Sat)

King's Arms

PUB

34 📍 MAP P44, B5

A mere 400 years old, the 'King' in question being James I, the self-styled 'brainiest pub' in Oxford is owned by Wadham College and run by Fullers brewery. Drop in and see how its predominantly academic clientele impresses you. Prints, memorabilia and photos – Prince Charles pulling a pint, the (late) Queen Mother drinking one – testify to its long history. (📞01865-242369; www.kingsarmsoxford.co.uk; 40 Holywell St; ⏱10.30am-midnight; 🛜)

Jericho Coffee Traders

COFFEE

35 📍 MAP P44, F3

Usually busy with students enjoying fine coffee and slabs of home-made cake, central Oxford's friendliest independent coffee house is an intimate, wood-panelled space. A single giant coffee table and low benches fill the tiny, sociable back room. This local roastery's original three-wheeled Vespa van spends most of its time at the Botanic Gardens these days. (📞07879 400163; www.facebook.com/jerichocoffeetraders; 105 High St; ⏱8.30am-5.30pm Mon-Fri, from 9am Sat, 10am-5pm Sun; 🛜)

Thirsty Meeples

CAFE

36 📍 MAP P44, C3

In the UK's original, and still Oxford's only, board-game cafe, paying £5 (£7 if you don't eat or drink) lets you play as many games as you like for three hours, choosing from over 2500 titles, and guided by expert staff. It serves everything from coffee, tea and shakes to beer, cider and cocktails, plus good pies, sandwiches and cakes. (📞01865-244247; www.thirstymeeples.co.uk; 99 Gloucester Green; ⏱11am-midnight Mon-Fri, from 9am Sat, to 11pm Sun; 🛜♿)

Varsity Club

COCKTAIL BAR

37 📍 MAP P44, E3

At this sleekly minimalist rooftop cocktail bar, spectacularly located in the town centre, you can sip fruity cocktails (£7 to £10) while soaking up sensational views across Oxford's dreaming spires. Heaters, blankets and canopies keep things cosy in colder weather, while lounges and dance spaces sprawl across three floors below. (📞01865-248777; www.tvcoxford.co.uk; 9 High St; ⏱noon-midnight; 🛜)

Bear Inn

PUB

38 📍 MAP P44, E4

Oxford's oldest pub – there's been a pub here since 1242 – the creaky old Bear requires almost everyone to stoop while passing from room to room. An ever-expanding collection of ties, framed and fading behind glass, covers walls and ceilings alike. Affiliated with Fuller's brewery, it usually offers interesting guest ales, plus basic pub grub. There's live jazz on Tuesday. (☏01865-728164; www.bearoxford. co.uk; 6 Alfred St; ⏰11am-11pm Mon-Thu, to midnight Fri & Sat, 11.30am-10.30pm Sun)

Three Goats Heads   PUB

39 🚇 MAP P44, D3

For some of the best (and cheapest!) real ale in town, head to this old-fashioned split-level pub, which exclusively serves beer from Sam Smith's brewery in Yorkshire, and holds no truck with new-fangled nonsense like music or TVs (or websites!). The upstairs bar offers carpets and dark-wood panelling, while the weekend-only Cellar Bar below has bare floors and green tiles. (☏01865-721523; 3-5 St Michael's St; ⏰noon-11pm Mon-Sat, to 10.30pm Sun)

George Street Social   BAR

40 🚇 MAP P44, D3

This sprawling central bar-restaurant offers a full food menu that centres on an all-day brunch, but the key to its essential identity lies in the latter half of its motto: 'eat, drink and be social'. For students, it's a heaven-sent central spot to meet friends and linger over coffee in the daytime, craft beers and cocktails at night. (☏01865-204735; www.georgestreet social.com; 36 New Inn Hall St; ⏰8am-11pm Mon-Fri, from 9am Sat & Sun; 📶)

The Grapes   PUB

41 🚇 MAP P44, D3

You've got to laugh! This gloriously authentic century-old pub stripped out its lovely old fittings a few years ago, reinvented itself as a hip modern bar called 'Beerd'...and fell completely flat. So they put everything back, and The Grapes is once again a cracking spot for a drink, albeit now serving craft beers as well as draught ales. (☏01865-793380; www.thegrapesoxford.com; 7 George St; ⏰11am-11pm Mon-Thu, to midnight Fri & Sat, to 10.30pm Sun)

Missing Bean   COFFEE

42 🚇 MAP P44, A6

Usually packed with students hunched over their laptops, this busy central coffee bar was inspired by Australia's independent cafe scene, and benefits from its East Oxford roastery, which holds another branch (p75). If you're not feeling crazy for caffeine, opt for some loose-leaf tea or a smoothie instead. Fresh muffins, flapjacks, cakes and filled ciabattas make it a handy lunchtime stop. (☏01865-794886; www.themissingbean.co.uk; 14 Turl St; ⏰8am-6pm Mon-Fri, 9am-6.30pm Sat, 10am-5.30pm Sun; 📶)

White Horse   PUB

43 🚇 MAP P44, A5

Every inch the quintessential old English pub, this tiny 16th-century inn was a favourite retreat for TV detective Inspector Morse, and attracts Morse devotees in droves.

Still a great place for a quiet afternoon pint of whatever guest ale happens to be on, it does get pretty crowded in the evenings. And don't bother with the food. (📞01865-204801; www.whitehorseoxford.co.uk; 52 Broad St; ⏱noon-11pm)

Entertainment

Oxford Playhouse THEATRE

44 ⭐ MAP P44, D2

Oxford's main stage for quality drama also hosts an impressive selection of touring music, dance and theatre performances. The Burton Taylor Studio often features quirky student productions and other innovative pieces. (📞01865-305305; www.oxfordplayhouse.com; Beaumont St)

Cellar LIVE MUSIC

45 ⭐ MAP P44, D3

There's live music or DJs most nights at this independent venue, covering the entire gamut of genres from indie rock to reggae, hip-hop, grime and downright disco. (📞01865-244761; www.cellaroxford.co.uk; Frewin Ct, off Cornmarket St; £3-10; ⏱hours vary, usually 7pm-late; 📶)

Shopping

Blackwell's BOOKS

46 🅰 MAP P44, B5

The most famous bookshop in the most studenty of cities, Blackwell's is, with its vast range of literature, treatises and guilty pleasures, a book-lover's dream. Be sure to visit the basement Norrington

Blackwell's

Creation Theatre

This ambitious **theatre company** (📞01865-766266; www.creationtheatre.co.uk) produces highly original shows – often Shakespeare, but also anything from *Dracula* to *The Wind in the Willows* – that are bursting with magic, quirk and special effects. It then performs them in all sorts of non-traditional venues, including city parks, the Westgate Shopping Centre, various colleges and Oxford Castle.

Room, an immense inverted step pyramid, lined with 3 miles of shelves, hailed in the Guinness Book of Records as the largest book-selling room in the world. (📞01865-792792; www.blackwells.co.uk; 48-51 Broad St; ⏰9am-6.30pm Mon & Wed-Sat, from 9.30am Tue, 11am-5pm Sun)

Westgate Shopping Centre

MALL

47 🔒 MAP P44, D5

Originally built in 1972 on the site of Oxford's medieval West Gate, this enormous mall expanded in 2017. Like Alice it seems just to keep on growing, with around 100 big-name shops including a large John Lewis department store, plus indoor golf and a cinema. Several of the smart, contemporary chain restaurants on the top floor have

Covered Market

WANG SING / SHUTTERSTOCK ©

outdoor roof-terrace seating. (📞01865-263600; www.westgate oxford.co.uk; Castle St; 🕐shops 10am-8pm Mon-Fri, from 9am Sat, 11am-5pm Sun, restaurants stay open longer hours; 📶)

Hoyle's   TOYS

48 🅐 MAP P44, G3

This charming shop sells games of every kind and age, from the latest board games – including bestsellers such as *Ticket To Ride* and *Dreaming Spires*, set in Oxford – to mahogany roulette wheels. For visitors of a certain age, its collection of vintage 1960s boxed games is a sure-fire exercise in nostalgia. (📞01865-203244; www.hoylesonline. com; 71 High St; 🕐9.30am-6pm Mon-Sat, 11.30am-6pm Sun)

Objects of Use   HOMEWARES

49 🅐 MAP P44, A6

The name says it all: this fascinating and quaint shop is piled high with useful household objects and tools to make each day easier. Everything is firstly functional, but most are also beautifully designed using sturdy natural materials. Lose yourself in the brush collection, eye up the pristine stationery or swoon at the charming crockery. (📞01865-241705; www. objectsofuse.com; 7 Lincoln House, Market St; 🕐10am-5pm Mon-Sat, 11am-4pm Sun)

Covered Market   MARKET

A treasure trove of traditional butchers, fishmongers, cobblers, florists, barbers, coffee bars, restaurants and independent shops, Oxford's 250-year-old Covered Market (see 22 ✕ Map p44, A6), tucked away off-street in the very heart of the city, is the place to go for everything from Sicilian sausage and tie-dye T-shirts to fancy flowers and wacky hats. (www. oxford-coveredmarket.co.uk; Market St; 🕐8am-5pm Mon-Sat, 10am-4pm Sun; 👪)

Alice's Shop   GIFTS & SOUVENIRS

50 🅐 MAP P44, E5

This tiny 500-year-old shop was operating as a grocery – and managed by a sheep – when Lewis Carroll's Alice popped in. Opposite Carroll's Christ Church home, it now sells *Alice in Wonderland* souvenirs from jigsaws to jewellery. (📞01865-240336; www.aliceinwon derlandshop.com; 83 St Aldate's; 🕐9.30am-6pm, to 6.30pm Jul & Aug)

Walking Tour 🥾

A Riverside Stroll in Central Oxford

Few cities can match Oxford for such glorious countryside so close to its centre. The riverside meadows just outside the city's long-vanished medieval walls have always belonged to wealthy colleges, which have never needed to build on them. Today's visitors can simply step away from the city streets to enjoy an idyllic stroll along delightful rural footpaths.

Walk Facts
Start Christ Church
End Grove Deer Park
Length 2.5 miles; two hours

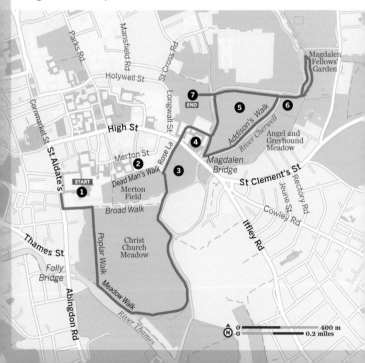

❶ Christ Church

From august **Christ Church** (p36), follow tree-lined **Poplar Walk** south to the Thames, then turn downstream along the riverfront **Meadow Walk**. You're now separated from Christ Church by lush **Christ Church Meadow**, grazed by longhorn cattle.

❷ Merton College

The footpath curves beside the Cherwell to meet Broad Walk. Straight ahead, the long, high wall of **Merton College** (p47) parallels the ancient city wall. Oxford's medieval Jewish community had to bury their dead outside the walls, so their funerals followed **Dead Man's Walk** outside.

❸ Botanic Garden

Oxford's former Jewish cemetery has for four centuries served as the **Botanic Garden** (p69). Add an optional half-mile to your walk if you fancy admiring its greenhouses of rare plants, and relaxing in its tranquil spaces.

❹ Magdalen College

Pay to enter **Magdalen College** (p66), and head through the stunning 15th-century cloisters. Author CS Lewis lived and taught in Magdalen, and the grotesque carvings here reappeared in his *Chronicles of Narnia*.

❺ Water Meadow

Magdalen has left the banks of the Cherwell untouched, as open countryside, for almost six centuries. A gloriously bucolic footpath, **Addison's Walk**, takes just under a mile to loop around the triangular islet of the Water Meadow. In late April, you may spot the purple or white flowers of the ultra-rare snakeshead fritillary.

❻ Bat Willow Meadow

To mark Magdalen's 550th anniversary, in 2008, Mark Wallinger's sculpture **Y**, resembling a two-dimensional tree, was installed in Bat Willow Meadow. Immediately south, **Angel and Greyhound Meadow** (p67) was named for two long-vanished coaching inns that pastured horses here. The secluded **Fellows' Garden** (p67), beyond, holds an idyllic pond.

❼ Grove Deer Park

Spare a glance as you head back to the high street for the **Grove Deer Park** (p67). If you're here between July and early December, you may have encountered the college's own herd of deer browsing in the riverside meadows; before that, to spare the fritillaries, they're here in the Grove.

Explore ✦

Cowley Road & Southeast Oxford

Both magnificent Magdalen College and the Botanic Garden – beside the Cherwell north and south of Magdalen Bridge respectively – are major attractions, offering sumptuous riverfront strolls. Oxford's southeastern quadrant beyond, though, is primarily residential. The main reason to venture across the bridge is to enjoy its student-led nightlife and dining.

As you can only visit Magdalen College (p66) after lunch during the university year, aim to spend an afternoon and evening in this neighbourhood. Allow an hour to savour the Botanic Garden (p69), more like two to wander Magdalen's wildflower-filled meadows and overgrown islands. En route, you'll see punts lined up at Magdalen Bridge (p69); if you want to try punting afterwards, why not drop in? Then enjoy a classic Cowley Rd evening, starting with dinner at Spiced Roots (p70) or the Magdalen Arms (p71). If it's Thursday, make a beeline for the Catweazle Club (p75); otherwise check out the O2 Academy (p75), or drink cocktails at Café Tarifa (p74) or Moya (p72).

Getting There & Around

🚶 Cowley Rd's nightlife is concentrated a few minutes' walk southeast of the centre, across Magdalen Bridge. This area is too far to walk from Oxford's train station.

🚌 Frequent services on route 5 connect Cowley Rd with the train station, via the city centre. Routes 3, 3A and 3B run between Iffley Rd and central Oxford.

Cowley Road & Southeast Oxford Map on p68

Facade of Magdalen College (p66) ANDY TAN HONG WEI / SHUTTERSTOCK ©

Top Sights
Magdalen College

Behind its high walls, and beyond its elegant Victorian gateway and medieval buildings, Magdalen College luxuriates in a hidden world of woodlands, river walks and manicured lawns. Established in 1458 by William Waynflete, Bishop of Winchester, it's among Oxford's richest and dreamiest colleges. Notable students have included CS Lewis, Oscar Wilde, Edward VIII, TE Lawrence 'of Arabia' and Cardinal Wolsey.

⊙ **MAP P68, A3**

☎ 01865-276000

www.magd.ox.ac.uk

High St

adult/child £6/5

⊙ 10am-7pm late Jun-late Sep, 1pm-dusk or 6pm late Sep-late Jun

Great Tower

The foundation stone of the Great Tower, which looms above Magdalen's original gateway, was laid on 9 August 1492, two months before Columbus reached the Americas. Standing 44m tall, it's where the college choir – also over 500 years old – sings *Hymnus Eucharisticus* at 6am on 1 May, to launch the May Day festivities.

The Cloisters

Magdalen's 15th-century cloisters, north of the college chapel, are decorated with sinister scowling grotesques, which no doubt stimulated the imagination of Magdalen don CS Lewis, who peopled his fictitious Narnia with similar stone statues. Also known as 'hieroglyphics', they were originally painted in bright colours. Some lucky undergraduates now live in the surrounding upper-level rooms.

The Meadows

Across a footbridge, and named for playwright Joseph Addison (1672–1719), Addison's Walk circles the delightful Water Meadow, on a triangular island in the Cherwell. Cross another bridge to reach Angel and Greyhound Meadow – the green tract that looks so enticing from Magdalen Bridge – smaller Bat Willow Meadow, and the secluded Fellows' Garden upstream.

Grove Deer Park

Magdalen's herd of deer – originally there was one animal per student – usually graze in the idyllic Grove Deer Park in winter and spring, then move to the riverside meadows between July and early December. King Charles I stationed his artillery here during the Civil War.

★ Top Tips

o Always pronounce Magdalen as 'mawd-lin', an affectation that stems from medieval French.

o Between late September and late June Magdalen only welcomes visitors in the afternoon.

o Come mid- to late April to see purple or white blooms of snakeshead fritillaries in the Water Meadow.

o The statues in the cloister are grotesques, not gargoyles; a gargoyle has a water spout in its mouth.

✕ Take a Break

The nearest spot for a snack, the Grand Café (p54), claims to be England's oldest coffee house.

The restaurants and bars of Cowley Rd, including the excellent Spiced Roots (p70), lie just across Magdalen Bridge.

| A | B | C | D |

1

St Cross Rd

Manor Rd

St Catherine's College

N 0 ___ 400 m
0 ___ 0.2 miles

For reviews see	
◉ Top Sights	p66
◉ Sights	p69
✷ Eating	p70
✷ Drinking	p74
✷ Entertainment	p75

2

Longwall St

Grove Deer Park

Water Meadow

Magdalen Fellows' Garden

Marston Rd

Addison's Walk

Y Sculpture

Bat Willow Meadow

Headington Rd

Magdalen College

High St

1 ◉

Rose La

2 Magdalen Bridge Boathouse

Angel and Greyhound Meadow

South Park

3

1 ◉ Botanic Garden

12

St Clement's St

7

11 ✷

8 ✷

10 ✷

Jeune St

Rectory Rd

Cross St

Morrell Ave

Magdalen College School

Iffley Rd

14

17

Princes St

Union St

East Ave

4

River Cherwell

4 ✷ **15** ✷

13 ✷

Temple St

Stockmore St

Marston St

Cowley Rd

3 ◉

Cyclo Analysts

18 ✷

James St

5

Christ Church Meadow

Bullingdon Rd

St Mary's Rd

Leopold St

Henley St

Hurst Rd

Aston St

Stanley Rd

6 ✷

Magdalen Rd

Jackdaw Lane

6

River Thames

Stratford St

Chester St

9 ✷

Warwick St

Iffley Rd

16 ✷

5

| A | B | C | D |

Sights

Botanic Garden GARDENS

1 ⊙ MAP P68, A3

Stretching beside the River Cherwell, Oxford's small, peaceful botanic garden was founded in 1621 for the study of medicinal plants. The oldest of its kind in England, it remains a department of the university, and is run more for research than for display. It's a lovely spot though, where greenhouses and open beds hold 'Plants That Changed The World' including potatoes, pineapples and cannabis. A riverside van sells coffee and snacks.

Near the river at its southern end you'll find the bench that Lyra and her extra-universal lover Will vow to visit once a year in Phillip Pullman's *His Dark Materials*. (📞01865-610305; www.botanic-garden.ox.ac.uk; High St; adult/child £5.45/free; ⏱9am-6pm, last admission 5.15pm May-Aug, noon-5pm Mon, 9am-5pm Tue-Sun, last admission 4.15pm Mar & Apr, 9am-5pm, last admission 3.15pm Sep-Feb)

Magdalen Bridge Boathouse BOATING

2 ⊙ MAP P68, A3

Right beside Magdalen Bridge, this boathouse is the most central location to hire a punt, chauffeured or otherwise. From here you can either head downstream around the Botanic Garden and Christ Church Meadow, or upstream around Magdalen Deer Park. You can also hire

Botanic Garden

The Cars of Cowley

Oxford isn't all about the university. It's also a centre for the British automotive industry. The man responsible was William Morris (1877–1963) – not the Arts and Crafts aesthete, in fact quite the reverse.

A working-class boy, Morris ran a bicycle-repair business from his family home off Iffley Rd, and was also a racing cyclist. Switching to repairing cars, he bought up land in Cowley so he could make them too. The first Morris Oxford, nicknamed the Bullnose (short for 'bullet nose') and priced at £175, appeared in 1913.

The UK equivalent of Henry Ford, Morris introduced assembly-line mass production to Britain. His booming Cowley operations attracted workers from all over Britain, and transformed the social make-up of Oxford. By the time the Mini appeared, in 1959, Morris' company had been swallowed up into the British Motor Corporation. One of his former factories, though, now Plant Oxford, still employs 4500 workers, and at time of writing was expected to start producing an all-electric Mini in 2019.

Morris himself became Lord Nuffield, and endowed a new Oxford college, Nuffield College.

---

rowboats and pedalos. (☑01865-202643; www.oxfordpunting.co.uk; High St; chauffeured 4-person punts per 30min £32, punt rental per hour £22; ☺9.30am-dusk Feb-Nov)

Cyclo Analysts BICYCLE HIRE

 3 ◉ MAP P68, C4

Sells, repairs and rents out bikes, including hybrids. (☑01865-424444; www.cycloanalysts.com; 150 Cowley Rd; per day/week from £10/36; ☺9am-6pm Mon-Sat)

Eating

Spiced Roots CARIBBEAN ££

 4 ✖ MAP P68, B4

From black rice with pomegranates to oxtail with mac cheese and plantains – and, of course, spicy jerk chicken – everything is just perfection at this flawless new Caribbean restaurant. There are plenty of vegetarian options too, as well as curried fish or goat, while adding a cocktail or two from the thatched rum bar is pretty much irresistible. (☑01865-249888; www.spicedroots.com; 64 Cowley Rd; mains £12-17.50; ☺6-10pm Tue & Wed, noon-3pm & 6-10pm Thu-Sat, noon-8pm Sun; ✐)

Magdalen Arms

BRITISH ££

5 ✗ MAP P68, C6

A mile beyond Magdalen Bridge, this extra-special neighbourhood gastropub has won plaudits from the national press. A friendly, informal spot, it offers indoor and outdoor space for drinkers, and dining tables further back. From vegetarian specials such as broad-bean tagliatelle to the fabulous sharing-size steak-and-ale pie – well, it's a stew with a suet-crust lid, really – everything is delicious, with gutsy flavours.

On the first Saturday of each month it holds a flea market outside, starting at 9.30am. (☎01865-243159; www.magdalenarms.co.uk; 243 Iffley Rd; mains £14-42; ☺5-11pm Mon, from 10am Tue-Sat, 10am-10.30pm Sun; ☑ ☑)

Oli's Thai

THAI ££

6 ✗ MAP P68, D6

This tiny Thai restaurant is a bit of a trek from town, a mile down Iffley Rd, but it's absolutely worth the effort. The short menu changes frequently, with standouts including turmeric prawns and pork belly with rice. Tables, especially on the sunny terrace, get booked up months in advance, but they usually squeeze in a few walk-ins. (☎01865-790223; www.olisthai. com; 38 Magdalen Rd; mains £12-15; ☺noon-2.30pm & 5-10pm Tue-Fri, noon-3pm Sat)

Magdalen Arms

STANISLAV HALCIN / ALAMY STOCK PHOTO ©

Coconut Tree
SRI LANKAN ££

7 ✖ MAP P68, C3

Just supposing 'Sri Lankan tapas' was actually a thing, this wildly popular bar-restaurant would be the best place to get it. What it really serves is small helpings of street food, including hoppers – bowl-shaped coconut-milk pancakes filled with rich sauces – lots of vegetarian options, including soya meatballs, and meat dishes such as slow cooked goat curry, plus two-for-£10 'cocotails'. (☑ 01865-421865; www.thecoconut -tree.com; 76 St Clement's St; small portions £3-8; ☺ noon-midnight Mon-Thu, to 1am Fri & Sat, to 10pm Sun; ✈)

Moya
SLOVAKIAN ££

8 ✖ MAP P68, B4

While Slovakian food has yet to sweep the foodie world, this little evening-only place has a lot of local fans. Vegetarians love the *halusky* dumplings, served with four kinds of mushrooms or sauerkraut, while the goulash is available with purple beans if you don't fancy beef. Give them half a chance and they'll also ply you with killer cocktails. (☑ 01865-200111; www.moya-oxford.co.uk; 97 St Clement's St; mains £10-14; ☺ 5.30pm-1am Tue-Thu, to 2am Fri & Sat; ✈)

The Chester
PUB FOOD ££

9 ✖ MAP P68, C6

Is The Chester a pub or a restaurant? Clearly it's both, with its busy beer garden, but the main reason visitors venture to this residential backstreet is because it serves Oxford's definitive roast on Sundays – beef for £13, a whole chicken to share for £33 – and a legendary steak platter otherwise, costing from £32 for two diners. (☑ 01865-790438; www.facebook. com/thechesteroxford; 19 Chester St; mains £12-18; ☺ noon-11pm Mon & Wed-Sat, from 5pm Tue, noon-10pm Sun; P 🛜 ♿ 🐾)

Kazbar
TAPAS ££

10 ✖ MAP P68, B4

As sultry as it is stylish, this energetic Moroccan-inspired bar-restaurant – a spin-off from nearby Café Coco – features hanging lanterns, draped fabrics, low lighting, warm colours and a fun, fresh vibe. A fashionable crowd sips cocktails and tucks into superb Spanish and North African tapas, perhaps hummus dips, chilli-prawns or cheese platters. Reservations for groups of eight or more only. (☑ 01865-202920; www. kazbar.co.uk; 25-27 Cowley Rd; tapas £3.70-10; ☺ 5pm-midnight Mon-Thu, 5pm-12.30am Fri, noon-12.30am Sat, to 11pm Sun; ✈)

Café Coco
MEDITERRANEAN £

11 ✖ MAP P68, B4

Decorated with classic posters, warm yellow walls and chunky mirrors – not to mention the plaster-cast clown – this Cowley Rd veteran is especially popular for brunch. Its global menu ranges from 'healthy' and cooked breakfasts to pizzas, salads, burgers, pastas, mezze platters, Mediterranean mains and zingy fresh juices. Or just swing by for cocktails (happy hour 5pm to 7.30pm). (☑01865-200232; www.cafecoco. co.uk; 23 Cowley Rd; breakfast £5-9, mains £7.50-15; ☺10am-midnight Mon-Thu, to 12.30am Fri & Sat, to 10pm Sun; ☑)

Rusty Bicycle
GASTROPUB £

This funky neighbourhood pub (see 6 ☒ Map p68, D6), tucked off Iffley Rd a mile out of town and brought to you by the people responsible for Jericho's Rickety Press (p85), serves top-notch burgers and pizzas, along with excellent local beers. (☑01865-435298; www. therustybicycle.com; 28 Magdalen Rd;

mains £6.50-12; ☺9am-11pm Sun-Thu, to midnight Fri & Sat; ☎)

Cuttlefish
SEAFOOD ££

12 ☒ MAP P68, B3

Whether your taste in seafood is for cod and chips (£11) or opulent mixed platters (from £38 for two), this bright, open Spanish-flavoured bistro will surely fit the bill. During the day it also serves brunch-y items such as eggs Benedict, and it offers burgers too, but it's fish dishes like the succulent, jet-black, squid-ink spaghetti seafood that'll bring you back. (☑01865-243003; www.cuttlefish oxford.co.uk; 36 St Clement's St; mains £11-19; ☺11am-10.30pm Mon-Sat, 10am-9.30pm Sun)

Goulash with sour cream

Roger Bannister & the Four-Minute Mile

Arguably the only time that Iffley Rd has figured in world history came shortly after 6pm on 8 May 1954, when Roger Bannister became the first man to run a mile in less than four minutes.

A former Oxford student, studying at medical school in London, Bannister came up on the train from Paddington that morning. The race, at the Iffley Rd track, didn't go entirely to plan. Behind the pace after his third lap, he raced the final circuit in 59 seconds, to achieve a time of three minutes 59.4 seconds.

The record made international headlines. During his distinguished later career, though, Bannister dismissed suggestions that breaking the four-minute barrier had been considered impossible. His fellow athletes had held the target very much in sight, much like today's aim of running a sub-two-hour marathon. Bannister held the record for just 46 days, and retired from running later that year.

The mile isn't often run these days. The current record was set in 1999, when Moroccan Hicham el Guerrouj ran it in three minutes 43.13 seconds.

Atomic Burger BURGERS ££

13 ⊗ MAP P68, C4

From Spiderman clinging to the ceiling on down, every inch here is smothered in pop-culture memorabilia. Standouts among its flavour-packed burgers include the Dead Elvis, the Boris Karloff, and the legendary £27.50 Fallout, a triple burger stack with triple cheese, triple jalapenos and terrifying ghost-chilli hot sauce. Its other outlet, Atomic Diner at 247 Cowley Rd, serves pizzas as well. (☏01865-790855; www.atomicburger. co.uk; 92 Cowley Rd; mains £9-17; ☺11.30am-10.30pm; ♟)

Drinking

Café Tarifa BAR

Inspired by the eponymous Spanish kitesurfing centre, this low-key lounge spot (see 4 ⊗ Map p68, B4) is big on neo-Moorish style, with cushioned booths, low-slung tables, tile-patterned sinks and cushy beanbags. There's a wide selection of cocktails, plus a menu of tapas and Mediterranean snacks, movie nights and live music. (☏01865-256091; www. cafe-tarifa.co.uk; 56-60 Cowley Rd; ☺5pm-midnight Mon-Thu, to 1am Fri, 10am-1am Sat, 10am-11pm Sun; ☎)

Big Society   PUB

14 🚌 MAP P68, C4

Revamped to meet the needs of students – table football, table tennis, cheap food, hand-pumped ales and the latest craft beers – rather than the car workers who traditionally lived along Cowley Rd, this big old corner pub is a major start- or end-the-night landmark on the Cowley Rd drinking scene. Tuesday night is quiz night. (📞01865-792755; www.bigsocietyoxford.com; 95 Cowley Rd; ⏰noon-midnight Sun-Thu, to 2am Fri & Sat; 📶)

Peloton Espresso   CAFE

15 🚌 MAP P68, B4

Celebrating cycling culture in all its forms, this cool modern coffee shop pulls in caffeine fiends with its stripped-back, bare-white decor, easygoing atmosphere and top-quality espresso. (📞01865-248808; www.facebook.com/peloton espresso; 76 Cowley Rd; ⏰8am-6pm Mon-Fri, from 9am Sat, from 10am Sun; 📶)

Missing Bean   CAFE

16 🚌 MAP P68, D6

Check out the artisanal roastery that's responsible for one of Oxford's favourite cafes, then pause over a flat white before grabbing a bag of the house roast for the road. From Magdalen Bridge, head a mile along Iffley Rd, then turn left onto Magdalen Rd. (📞01865-794886; www.themissingbean.co.uk; 1 Newtec Pl, Magdalen Rd; ⏰7am-2pm Tue-Fri, from 10am Sat)

Entertainment

Catweazle Club   LIVE MUSIC

17 ⭐ MAP P68, C4

This legendary weekly open-mic night has migrated from venue to venue. Now firmly ensconced at the East Oxford Social Club, it features an ever-changing panoply of musicians, poets, writers and all sorts of bohemian performers. (www.catweazleclub.com; East Oxford Social Club, 44 Princes St; cover £6; ⏰8pm Thu)

O2 Academy   LIVE MUSIC

18 ⭐ MAP P68, D5

Oxford's busiest club and live-music venue (previously known as the Venue and the Zodiac, way back when) hosts everything from big-name DJs and international touring artists to indie bands and hard rock. (📞01865-813500; www.academymusicgroup.com/o2academy oxford; 190 Cowley Rd)

Explore ⊕

Jericho & the Science Area

Built to house labourers during the Industrial Revolution, but now a prime residential neighbourhood, Jericho is home to the unmissable Ashmolean Museum, as well as excellent restaurants and pubs. The Science Area to the east holds most of the university's science departments, plus the Natural History museum, bursting with dinosaurs, and the faintly dotty, always intriguing Pitt Rivers Museum.

These neighbourhoods are so close to central Oxford that it's easy to dip in as and when you like. That said, you can spend a great day exploring the Natural History (p84) and Pitt Rivers (p80) museums in the morning, and devoting the entire afternoon to the Ashmolean (p78). (Come back if you miss anything – it's free). Stop for lunch in the Ashmolean's Rooftop Restaurant (p86), or the venerable Lamb & Flag (p87), then spend the evening sampling Jericho's pubs – both the Old Bookbinders Ale House (p84) and the Rickety Press (p85) serve great food and drink.

Getting There & Around

🚶 All the museums hereabouts lie within a few minutes' walk of the city centre, while the Ashmolean is around 10 minutes on foot from Oxford's train station.

🚌 No direct bus connects central Oxford with the nightlife area around Walton St, but for some destinations it helps to catch 6 up St Giles, or 2 up Banbury Rd, from Magdalen St.

Jericho & the Science Area Map on p82

Museum of Natural History (p84) PRISMA BY DUKAS / GETTY IMAGES ©

Top Sights 📷
Ashmolean Museum

Only the British Museum in London can surpass the historical, archaeological and artistic treasures of Oxford's world-class Ashmolean. Each bright, spacious gallery of this magnificent neoclassical building holds some new marvel. Highlights range from the Alfred Jewel, a glorious golden teardrop created for Alfred the Great, to a lantern carried by Guy Fawkes, with strong connections throughout to Oxford itself.

◎ MAP P82, E5

☏ 01865-278000

www.ashmolean.org

Beaumont St

admission free

🕐 10am–5pm Tue–Sun, to 8pm last Fri of month

The Ashmolean Story

The Ashmolean was created in 1683, after Elias Ashmole (1617–92) presented Oxford University with 'rarities' collected by John Tradescant, world-roaming gardener to Charles I. The Ashmolean Story exhibition displays treasures gathered by Tradescant in Virginia in the 1630s, including a mantle said to have belonged to 'Chief Powhatan', father of Pocahontas, plus the hat worn by the judge who presided over the trial of Charles I.

The Art of the Ashmolean

Paolo Uccello's 1470 painting *The Hunt in the Forest* (pictured) is the acknowledged master-piece, but the Ashmolean's collection of fine art extends from Renaissance Italy to Japan. Look out for Michelangelo's red-chalk sketches for the Sistine Chapel; Hiroshige's woodblock prints; watercolours by Turner; and etchings by Goya.

Ancient World

You never know what you'll encounter next in the ground-floor 'Ancient World' galleries – stone reliefs and ivory panels from the Assyrian palace of Nimrud, erotic statues from Rome, or terracotta figurines from 6th-century Japan. One section covers pre-Roman Italy with Etruscan urns and miniature Bronze Age warriors.

Treasures from Knossos

The Ashmolean owes its extraordinary collection from Minoan Crete to former Keeper Sir Arthur Evans (1851–1941). The first to excavate the palace of Knossos, Evans called its culture 'Minoan', after legendary King Minos. Displays include artefacts he brought back, such as colossal storage jars, alongside dazzling frescoes.

★ **Top Tips**

○ Entry to the Ashmolean is free, so it makes sense to explore it in stages, spread over more than one visit.

○ The rooftop restaurant only stays open for dinner on Thursday, Friday and Saturday.

○ Check online before you visit, for details of the Ashmolean's ever-changing special, short-term exhibitions.

○ First-come, first-served guided tours, devoted to changing daily themes, set off at 1.15pm Tuesday to Saturday.

✕ **Take a Break**

The Ashmolean's own Rooftop Restaurant (p86), renowned for its fine food and a perfect spot for afternoon tea, is the obvious place to catch your breath between galleries.

Otherwise, the legendary Lamb & Flag (p87), beloved by JRR Tolkien and CS Lewis, is just up the road.

Top Sights 📷
Pitt Rivers Museum

If exploring a murky, mysterious cavern full of eccentric artefacts sounds like your idea of the perfect afternoon, welcome to the amulets-to-zithers extravaganza that's the Pitt Rivers museum. Dimly lit to protect its marvels, it centres on the anthropological collection of a Victorian general. A treasure-house of wonders, it's piled high with creaking cases and cabinets filled with extraordinary objects, laid out by theme rather than region.

◎ MAP P82, G3

☏ 01865-270927

www.prm.ox.ac.uk

South Parks Rd

admission free

🕐 noon-4.30pm Mon, from 10am Tue-Sun

The Court: Magic, Masks & Music

The ground floor is a veritable maze. Each wooden cabinet crowded into the central hall holds a 'typological display', like 'Smoking and Stimulants' or 'Treatment of Dead Enemies'. There's no chance you'll see everything, or even find anything you're looking for, but you'll have a good time trying. Much space is devoted to objects associated with ritual and magic, such as charms to protect from the evil eye. Fascinating music-making devices include a case of 'Drums and Voice Disguisers', and another of lamellaphones (wait and see!).

Lower Gallery: Tattoos, Tools & Toys

Despite the name, the Lower Gallery is upstairs, the lower of two balconies circling above the central hall. There's a generally gentler tone to its displays on puppets, toys, body decoration and jewellery. If you're of a nervous disposition, though, don't inspect 'Medicine and Surgery' too closely.

Cook-Voyage Collection

Artefacts gathered during the Pacific voyages of Captain James Cook (1728–79), displayed in the Lower Gallery, include a barkcloth mourners' costume from Tahiti. One group of items, donated by naturalist Joseph Banks to Christ Church in 1773, remained forgotten until 2002.

Upper Gallery: Shields, Spears & Samurai

While the Japanese samurai gear immediately catches the eye on the top floor, other amazing items include forbidding helmets from Bronze Age Greece, and even, filed under 'non-metal armour', a very spiky helmet from Kiribati in Oceania, made from the skin of a porcupine fish.

★ **Top Tips**

o The only entrance to the Pitt Rivers Museum is via the Natural History museum; try to allow time to visit that museum as well while you're here.

o Every Saturday morning at 11am the museum hosts free, family-oriented 'object handling' sessions.

o One firmly stoppered bottle is said to contain a witch; don't open it.

✗ **Take a Break**

The nearest place to the museum to get food or drink is the much-loved Lamb & Flag (p87) pub, 300yd west along Lamb & Flag Passage.

Turning right halfway along that narrow alleyway will bring you instead, after a similar distance, to the Parsonage Grill (p87), a classy hotel restaurant that also serves a formal afternoon tea.

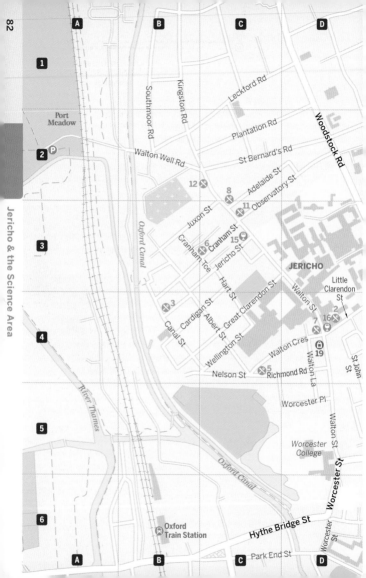

A B C D

1

Port
Meadow

2 P

Southmoor Rd

Kingston Rd

Leckford Rd

Plantation Rd

St Bernard's Rd

Woodstock Rd

Walton Well Rd

12 ✕ 8 ✕ Adelaide St

Observatory St

11

Oxford Canal

Juxon St

Cranham Tce

Cranham St

6 ✕

15 ?

Jericho St

3

Hart St

JERICHO

Little
Clarendon
St

Walton St

2

3 ✕

Cardigan St

Albert St

Great Clarendon St

Wellington St

7 ✕ 16 ?

19 🔒

Walton Cres

Walton La

St John St

Canal St

4

Nelson St

5 ✕ Richmond Rd

Worcester Pl

Walton St

River Thames

5

Worcester
College

Worcester St

Oxford Canal

Worcester St

6

Oxford
Train Station

Hythe Bridge St

A B C Park End St D

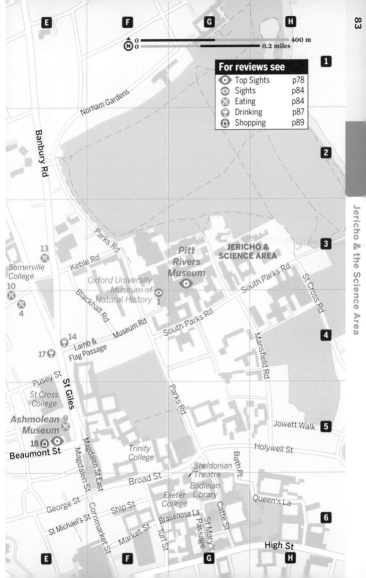

E F G H

For reviews see
- Top Sights p78
- Sights p84
- Eating p84
- Drinking p87
- Shopping p89

0 400 m
0 0.2 miles

Norham Gardens

Banbury Rd

Parks Rd

13

Somerville
College

10

4

Keble Rd

Oxford University
Museum of
Natural History

Blackhall Rd

1

Pitt
Rivers
Museum

JERICHO &
SCIENCE AREA

South Parks Rd

St Cross Rd

14

17

Lamb &
Flag Passage

Museum Rd

South Parks Rd

Mansfield Rd

Pusey St

St Cross
College

St Giles

Ashmolean
Museum

9

18

Beaumont St

Magdalen St East

Magdalen St

Parks Rd

Trinity
College

Jowett Walk

Holywell St

Broad St

Sheldonian
Theatre

Bodleian
Library

Bath Pl

Queen's La

George St

St Michael's St

Cornmarket St

Ship St

Market St

Exeter
College

Turl St

Brasenose La

St Mary's
Passage

Catte St

High St

E F G H

Sights

Oxford University Museum of Natural History   MUSEUM

1 MAP P82, F4

Housed in a glorious Victorian Gothic building, with cast-iron columns, flower-carved capitals and a soaring glass roof, this museum makes a superb showcase for some extraordinary exhibits. Specimens from all over the world include a 150-year-old Japanese spider crab, but it's the dinosaurs that really wow the crowds. As well as a towering T-rex skeleton – 'Stan', the second most complete ever found – you'll see pieces of Megalosaurus, which was in 1677 the first dinosaur ever mentioned in a written text.

A particular local favourite is the (stuffed) dodo that was immortalised by Lewis Carroll in *Alice in Wonderland*. The unfortunate bird was stunningly revealed in 2018 to have been shot in the head, rather than dying peacefully in captivity, as previously thought. (☎01865-272950; www.oum.ox.ac.uk; Parks Rd; admission free; ⏰10am-5pm; 👶)

The Local Press

Spare a glance as you stroll Walton St for the imposing headquarters of the **Oxford University Press**, a local landmark for almost 200 years; its presence has done much to shape Jericho's distinctive identity.

Eating

Natural Bread Company   BAKERY £

2 ✗ MAP P82, D4

An early-morning social centre for students from adjoining Somerville College, this small bakery-cafe is renowned for wonderful breads like the wheat-and-rye 'Brainy' and rich French pastries including the prune-packed Far Breton. Breakfast choices range from yoghurt and granola to black pudding baps, while for lunch you can get a thick soup or stew with a hunk of sourdough bread. (☎01865-302996; www.naturalbreadcompany.co.uk; 29 Little Clarendon St; mains £5-9; ⏰7.30am-4.30pm Mon-Sat, 8am-4pm Sun; 📶🌱)

Old Bookbinders Ale House   PUB, FRENCH £

3 ✗ MAP P82, B4

This charming neighbourhood pub is a hit with Jericho locals for its distinctive and very tasty line in French cuisine, including simple classics like beef stew, chicken with cream, and steak and chips. Best of all, it serves what it appetisingly calls 'a load of crepes' – delicious pancakes, with savoury fillings. Most customers tend to linger for a post-dinner pint. (☎01865-553549; www.old bookbinders.co.uk; 17-18 Victor St; mains £7-15.50; ⏰noon-11pm, kitchen

noon-2.15pm & 5.30-9.15pm Mon-Sat,
noon-7pm Sun; 🛜 ✈ 👫 🐾)

George & Davis

ICE CREAM £

4 ❌ MAP P82, E4

The original in a three-strong
chain of Oxford ice-cream cafes,
better known as G&Ds, this is
where they actually make the
stuff, with new flavours being
concocted all the time. If you don't
have a sweet tooth, content yourself with a £3 house-made bagel.
The cow-themed interior is casual
and friendly. (📞01865-516652;
www.gdcafe.com; 55 Little Clarendon
St; ice creams £2.40–5.60; ⏲8am-
midnight; 👫)

Al-Shami

LEBANESE £

5 ❌ MAP P82, C4

This long-standing Jericho
institution is a sure bet for tasty
and authentic Lebanese food. For
vegetarians especially, the wide
range of hot and cold meze – be
sure to try the fried cauliflower
dish *zahra maqlia* – makes a great
meal in itself, with set menus from
£15 per person, but it also offers
excellent charcoal-grilled lamb and
chicken. (📞01865-310066; www.
al-shami.co.uk; 25 Walton Cres; mains
£7-12; ⏲noon-midnight; ✈)

Rickety Press

GASTROPUB £

6 ❌ MAP P82, C3

Tucked away in the backstreets of
Jericho, this revamped gastropub
is something of a hipster haunt for

Museum of Natural History

its high-class brioche-bun burgers, wood-fired pizzas, artisan beers, cocktails, tasty snacks (quinoa and kale salad, cheese'n'truffle chips) and book-lined shelves. Weekend brunch options include favourites like the 'Boss Man' full English breakfast and chilli-smashed avocado. (📞01865-424581; www.thericketypress.com; 67 Cranham St; mains £6.50-12; ⏱kitchen noon-2.30pm & 6-9.30pm Mon-Fri, 10am-3pm & 6-9.30pm Sat & Sun)

Opera   MIDDLE EASTERN £

7 🍴 MAP P82, D4

This charming cafe's streetfront deck is a prime people-watching spot, though there's also a secluded soft-furnished snug downstairs. The menu has a strong Middle Eastern flavour, with breakfast choices including a Moroccan egg wrap as well as Jericho's obligatory avocado toast. Or just stop by for a coffee or fresh-squeezed juice and a slice of *basbousa*, a syrup-infused semolina cake. (📞01865-236140; www.facebook.com/operacafe; 31 Walton St; mains £5-8; ⏱8am-10pm Mon-Fri, 9am-8pm Sat & Sun; 🛜🖊👫👶)

Manos Café-Deli   GREEK £

8 🍴 MAP P82, C2

For home-cooked tastes of the Mediterranean, head for this Greek deli-restaurant, where you'll find the likes of spinach-and-feta tart, chicken or felafel souvlaki, plus a great selection of meze. The no-frills ground-floor cafe and

deli serves inexpensive wraps and salads, while the garden and downstairs dining room are a bit more relaxed. (📞01865-311782; www.manosfoodbar.com; 105 Walton St; mains £7-10; ⏱10.30am-9pm Mon-Thu, to 9.30pm Fri, 9.30am-10pm Sat, 11.30am-5pm Sun; 🖊)

Ashmolean Rooftop Restaurant   MODERN BRITISH ££

9 🍴 MAP P82, E5

Run by the Benugo chain, the Ashmolean's light-filled rooftop restaurant serves meticulous modern dishes such as black squid crusted cod or mustard-marinated lamb, with the two-/three-course lunch menu (£18/23), themed around a current exhibition, available until 7.30pm. Or come to enjoy afternoon tea on the outdoor terrace (£26 for two), savouring the views from a deckchair on the fake-grass 'lawn'. (📞01865-553823; www.ashmolean.org; Beaumont St; mains £13.50-20; ⏱10am-4.30pm Tue, Wed & Sun, to 10pm Thu-Sat; 🛜)

Pierre Victoire   FRENCH ££

10 🍴 MAP P82, E4

This much-loved little bistro has earned a sky-high local reputation for its scrupulously prepared array of classic dishes from all over France. From fish soup to risotto, snails to fondue, and mussels to roasted duck breast, everything is *magnifique*. There's a £25 three-course set dinner menu every night except Saturday, and an £11.50 two-course lunch every

Jericho & the Science Area Drinking

day except Sunday. (📞01865-316616; www.pierrevictoire.co.uk; 9 Little Clarendon St; mains £12-24; 🕐noon-2.30pm & 8-11pm Mon-Sat, noon-10pm Sun)

Branca   ITALIAN ££

11 🍴 MAP P82, C3

Big, bright and bustling, this glitzy Jericho favourite serves cool cocktails and savoury focaccia to complement elegant, well-prepped pizzas, pastas, risottos, and Italian meat and seafood grills. There's a good-value, two-course lunch/early dinner deal (£15.50), from noon to 7pm Monday to Thursday, noon to 5pm Friday and Saturday. It also runs the deli next door. (📞01865-556111; www.branca.co.uk; 110-111 Walton St; mains £11-17.50; 🕐10am-10pm Sun-Wed, to 10.30pm Thu-Sat)

Zheng   CHINESE, MALAYSIAN ££

12 🍴 MAP P82, C2

The ambience in this Jericho restaurant seems half big-city nightspot, half local takeout, but if you're partial to Asian flavours, something on its long, glossy Chinese-Malaysian menu will surely tickle your tastebuds. Apart from a handful of fish dishes, most mains – from crispy Singaporean prawns to spicy-as-all-hell Szechuan lamb – cost under £14, but vegetable sides will push the bill higher. (📞01865-558888; www.zhengoxford.co.uk; 82 Walton St; mains £9-22; 🕐noon-2.30pm & 5.30-10.45pm Mon & Wed-Fri, 5.30-10.45pm

Tue, noon-10.45pm Sat, noon-10.15pm Sun; 🛜🍴)

Parsonage Grill   BRITISH £££

13 🍴 MAP P82, E3

For a taste of old-Oxford formality with the feel of a gentlemen's club, dine amid this hotel restaurant's dark-wood panelling and original paintings. Its all-day menu features standards like lamb rump or sea bream fillet, while the two-/three-course (£18/23) weekday set lunch is served until 6pm. Afternoon tea in the spacious courtyard, whether 'very high' or 'very savoury', costs £25. (📞01865-310210; www.parsonagegrill.co.uk; Old Parsonage Hotel, 1-3 Banbury Rd; mains £18-33; 🕐noon-11pm; 🛜)

Drinking

Lamb & Flag   PUB

14 🍺 MAP P82, E4

This relaxed 17th-century tavern remains one of Oxford's nicest pubs for a sturdy pint or glass of wine. Thomas Hardy wrote (and set) parts of Jude the Obscure at these very tables, while CS Lewis and JRR Tolkien shifted their custom here in later years. The food's nothing special, but buying a pint helps fund scholarships at St John's College. (12 St Giles; 🕐noon-11pm Mon-Sat, to 10.30pm Sun; 🛜)

Raoul's   COCKTAIL BAR

A long-established local favourite, Jericho's finest retro-look bar (see 7 🍺 Map p82, D4) is renowned for its expertly mixed cocktails – typically priced at around £7.50, and infused with fresh fruit – along with its moody booths, laid-back lounge music, and 'watering can' sharing concoctions. (📞01865-553732; www.raoulsbar.com; 32 Walton St; 🕐4pm-midnight Sun-Tue, to 1am Fri & Sat)

Jericho Tavern PUB

15 🚇 MAP P82, C3

A sturdy four-square fixture on Jericho's main street, this veteran pub has benefitted from an appealing modern makeover, and now places a strong emphasis on serving craft beers from around the world, in kegs as well as bottles. Proud of having hosted early gigs by Radiohead and Supergrass, it still puts on regular live music. (📞01865-311775; www.thejerichooxford.co.uk; 56 Walton St; 🕐noon-11pm Sun-Wed, to midnight Thu-Sat)

Oxford Wine Café WINE BAR

16 🚇 MAP P82, D4

This fresh, sophisticated wine bar is popular with laptop-toting students and the after-work crowd. Choose from a fantastic array of world-spanning wines by the glass (from £3.50) or bottle, topped up with cheese, meats and dips (dishes £6 to £12). Why the early opening? Because like everywhere else in Jericho, it's filled first thing with locals topping up on caffeine. (📞01865-604334; www.oxfordwinecafe.co.uk; 32 Little Clarendon St; 🕐8.30am-11pm Mon-Thu, to midnight Fri, 10am-midnight Sat, 10am-10pm Sun; 🛜)

Eagle & Child PUB

17 🚇 MAP P82, E4

Affectionately nicknamed the 'Bird & Baby', and a favourite haunt of JRR Tolkien, CS Lewis and their fellow Inklings, this quirky, rambling pub dates from 1650.

A Punt, a Pint, and Plaice & Peas

If you fancy escaping the city for an afternoon's escapade beside, on, or even in the River Cherwell, both Jericho and the Science Area lie within a mile's walk of the idyllic **Cherwell Boathouse** (📞01865-515978; www.cherwellboathouse.co.uk; 50 Bardwell Rd; punt rental per hour Mon-Fri £17, Sat & Sun £19; 🕐10am-dusk mid-Mar–mid-Oct). In an irresistible riverside setting, the century-old Boathouse rents out punts, rowboats and canoes, while its **restaurant** (mains £18-22; 🕐noon-2.30pm & 6-9.30pm; 🖋) serves a fine menu of British standards such as lamb loin with peas or plaice with shrimp sauce.

Get there by heading north along Banbury Rd, then turning right onto Bardwell Rd, which dead-ends after around 750 yards.

Last Bookshop

Its narrow wood-panelled rooms still look great, and they're still serving decent real ales, but it's lost its way recently, and owners St John's College have announced an imminent, ominous-sounding makeover. (📞01865-302925; www.nicholsonspubs.co.uk/theeagleandchildoxford; 49 St Giles; ⏱11am-11pm Mon-Sat, noon-10.30pm Sun)

Shopping

Ashmolean Shop GIFTS & SOUVENIRS

18 🔒 MAP P82, E5

Appropriately enough, the shop at the Ashmolean reflects the scope and variety of Oxford's finest museum. William Morris would certainly approve – everything is either beautiful or useful, and most are both. From postcards of Japanese woodblock prints to Juan Gris mirrors and Cressida Bell–designed notepaper, it's the perfect place to pick up classy gifts and souvenirs. (📞01865-278000; www.ashmolean.org; Beaumont St; ⏱10am-5pm Tue-Sun, to 8pm last Fri of month)

Last Bookshop BOOKS

19 🔒 MAP P82, D4

Booklovers beware! This enticing little Jericho shop can easily swallow an hour of your time. Specialising in remainders and discounted stocks, largely from academic publishers, which it sells at £3 each or two for £5, it also serves coffee and snacks, with rickety tables on the little pavement terrace out front. (📞01865-554488; 25 Walton St; ⏱10am-7pm Mon-Sat, to 6.30pm Sun)

Walking Tour 🥾

Port Meadow

A wonderful country jaunt on Oxford's very doorstep, this 5.5-mile loop leads out across wild, wide-open Port Meadow, and back along a blissful Thames-side footpath. En route, it takes in remarkable ancient sites as well as two of Oxford's best-loved rural pubs. Setting off from either Jericho or central Oxford adds 1 or 2 miles respectively to the total round-trip.

Walk Facts
Start Walton Well Rd
End Walton Well Rd
Length 5.5 miles; two hours

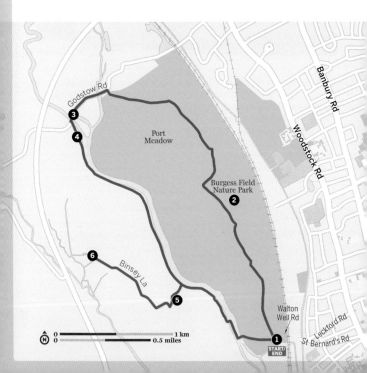

❶ Walton Well Road

Marshy, riverine Port Meadow, northwest of Jericho, has been communal grazing land for at least a thousand years, and it's still roamed by cows and horses. Never ploughed, and as pristine a landscape as any in England, it's a treasure trove of rare plants. Wildfowl and ice-skaters alike congregate in winter, when large tracts freeze over.

❷ Burgess Field Nature Park

The paved path across Port Meadow ends half a mile along. Unless you're here in high summer, you may well prefer to avoid mud and puddles by detouring to your right, to pass through wooded Burgess Field. Tracks meander through successive copses, alive with bluebells in spring, before you re-enter Port Meadow after three-quarters of a mile.

❸ The Trout

Cut across Port Meadow's north-west corner, and cross a mill-stream to meet the Thames. The 400-year-old pub here, **The Trout** (☎01865-510930; www.thetroutoxford.co.uk; 195 Godstow Rd, Wolvercote; ⏰11am-11pm Mon-Fri, from 10am Sat, 10am-10.30pm Sun; 🛜), was a favourite haunt of TV's Inspector Morse. Its riverfront terrace – usually packed, and patrolled by peckish ducks – is a perfect spot for a pint. It's also renowned for its British cuisine – book ahead.

❹ Godstow Nunnery

Just across the Thames, only a ruined chapel remains of Godstow Nunnery, founded in 1145 by Ediva of Winchester. This being the furthest north you can row from Oxford, it's where Lewis Carroll stopped on 4 July 1862. Over a picnic on its rich lawns, he told Alice Liddell the story that became *Alice in Wonderland*.

❺ The Perch

The Thames Path heads south through lovely scenery, with trees fringing the riverbank. A mile along, an enchanting side path, punctuated by floral pergolas, leads to the thatched, 800-year-old **Perch** (☎01865-728891; www.the-perch.co.uk; Binsey Lane, Binsey; ⏰10.30am-11pm Mon-Sat, to 10.30pm Sun; 🅿🎠). The pub's huge willow-draped garden is a lovely place to drink, but summer crowds can mean a long wait for food.

❻ St Margaret of Antioch

Binsey's small 12th-century **church** (www.osneybenefice.org.uk; Binsey Lane, Binsey; ⏰daily, hours vary) stands half a mile west of the Perch, along a magnificent avenue of poplars. Pilgrims including Henry VIII once flocked here, drawn by the healing waters of **St Margaret's Well** – the 'Treacle Well' mentioned in *Alice in Wonderland*. Retrace your steps to the Thames, continue south, and you'll be directed back to Port Meadow across two footbridges.

Worth a Trip 🔭
Blenheim Palace

Blenheim Palace, a majestic baroque extrava-
ganza set in superbly landscaped grounds, was
given by Queen Anne to John Churchill, Duke of
Marlborough, in thanks for defeating the French
at the 1704 Battle of Blenheim (pronounced blen-
num). Just outside Woodstock, 8 miles northwest
of Oxford, it was designed by Sir John Vanbrugh
and Nicholas Hawksmoor, and completed in 1722.

📞 01993-810530

www.blenheimpalace.com

Woodstock

adult/child £26/14.50,
park & gardens only
£16/7.40

🕑 palace 10.30am-
5.30pm, park & gardens
9am-6.30pm or dusk

Inside the Palace

Beyond majestic oak doors, the palace is stuffed with statues, tapestries, sumptuous furniture, and enormous paintings. Visits start in the soaring Great Hall, adorned with images of the first duke. Highlights include the Blenheim Tapestries, commemorating the first duke's triumphs; the State Dining Room, with its *trompe l'œil* ceilings; and the magnificent Long Library, where the 56m-long ceiling was decorated by Nicholas Hawksmoor.

Churchill Exhibition

The Churchill Exhibition, downstairs, covers the life, work, paintings and writings of British prime minister Sir Winston Churchill. Grandson of the 7th duke and cousin of the 9th, he was born here in 1874, and is buried in the parish church in Bladon, 1.5 miles south.

The Untold Story

Upstairs, in the Untold Story, a phantom chambermaid leads visitors on audio-visual tours of tableaux depicting scenes from Blenheim's history. Each set of doors is on a timer, so once inside, you're committed to the full half-hour saga of illicit affairs and upstairs-downstairs intrigue.

The Estate

Parts of Blenheim's vast parklands were laid out by Lancelot 'Capability' Brown. Terraces outside the house hold fountains and sphinxes, while a minitrain runs to the Pleasure Gardens, equipped with yew maze, adventure playground and butterfly house. Longer strolls lead to an arboretum, a rose garden and Vanbrugh's Grand Bridge. At the Temple of Diana, Winston Churchill proposed to his future bride, Lady Clementine, on 10 August 1908.

Getting There

Stagecoach buses connect Blenheim Palace and Woodstock with Oxford (S3; £3.20, 30 minutes), Burford (233; £4.10, 45 minutes), Chipping Norton (S3; £4.10, 20 minutes) and Witney (233; £3.80, 30 minutes).

✕ Take a Break

The handsome town of Woodstock, alongside Blenheim Palace, holds plenty of restaurants, bakeries, cafes and pubs. The **King's Arms** (☑ 01993-813636; www.kingshotelwoodstock.co.uk; 19 Market St; mains £13-23.50; ⏱7-10am, noon-2.30pm & 6-9.30pm Mon-Fri, 8-10am, noon-2.30pm & 6-9.30pm Sat, 8-10am, noon-4pm & 6-9pm Sun; 🛜) is a large central gastro-pub where you can get anything from pub-grub standards such as burgers and fish and chips to more creative dishes such as pan-seared pollock with langoustines.

Cotswolds Regions

Chipping Campden (p107)
Arguably the Cotswolds' prettiest village, lined with glorious medieval mansions that glow in the afternoon sun.

Chipping Norton & the Central Cotswolds (p97)
Chipping Norton is a gateway to the Cotswolds. To the west lie the historic towns of Moreton-in-Marsh and Stow-on-the-Wold.

Broadway & the Northwest Cotswolds (p115)
Peaceful Broadway holds a fine museum, pubs and restaurants. Nearby Winchcombe is home to stunning Sudeley Castle.

Stratford-upon-Avon

Chipping Campden

Broadway

Chipping Norton

Blenheim Palace

London
Oxford
Airport

Burford

Cirencester

Oxford

Burford & the Southeast Cotswolds (p125)
Lively Burford is a great base for seeing quieter Northleach and exquisite little Bibury.

Cirencester & the Southwest Cotswolds (p135)
The largest Cotswolds town honours its Roman heritage in an excellent museum. Nearby, lovely Painswick boasts a celebrated garden.

Explore
the Cotswolds

No one's sure what the name means, but 'wolds' are rolling hills, while 'cots' might be 'cotes', or sheep pens. Undulating gracefully across six counties, the Cotswolds region is a delightful tangle of golden villages, thatched cottages, evocative churches and honey-coloured mansions.

Explore ◈

Chipping Norton & the Central Cotswolds

The handsome but slightly faded hilltop town of Chipping Norton guards the northeastern approach to the Cotswolds. Popularly known as 'Chippy', it centres on a market square that boasts stately Georgian buildings and old coaching inns plus a 19th-century town hall.

Allow a morning to explore, strolling past honey-tinged 17th-century almshouses to the wool-era St Mary's Church (p99), and pausing for lunch at Wild Thyme (p99) or coffee in Jaffe & Neal (p99). In the afternoon, venture out to Jacobean Chastleton House (p99) or the Rollright Stones (p101). Then spend a second day in the lively neighbouring towns of Stow-on-the-Wold (p104) – an appealing maze of a place – and grander-looking Moreton-in-Marsh (p103), squeezing in a drink or meal at the King's Head Inn (p104).

Getting There & Around

🚌 Stagecoach and/or Pulhams buses connect Chipping Norton with Oxford (route S3; £4.70, one hour), and Moreton-in-Marsh with Stow-on-the-Wold (route 801; £1.90, 10 minutes), Chipping Campden (route 1/2; £3.90, 50 minutes) and Broadway (route 1/2; £3.90, 30 minutes).

🚆 Moreton-in-Marsh has rail services from Oxford (£10.60, 35 minutes) and London Paddington (£14.50, 1½ hours).

Chipping Norton & Central Cotswolds Map on p102

Bliss Tweed Mill (p99) RICHARD SHEPPARD / ALAMY STOCK PHOTO ©

Top Sights 🔭
Chipping Norton

Situated in an area that's been inhabited since prehistoric times, the settlement of Chipping Norton dates back to the 12th century, and grew prosperous on the back of the thriving wool industry. Today it's still a lively market town, and has some interesting sights both within the town and nearby.

◎ **MAP P102, E3**

Chipping Norton is on the A44, 21 miles northwest of Oxford and 8 miles southeast of Moreton-in-Marsh.

St Mary's Church

A classic Cotswold wool church, **St Mary's**
(☏01608-646202; www.stmaryscnorton.com;
Church St; ⊙10am-dusk) has a magnificent
Perpendicular nave and clerestory, several
alabaster tombs and elegant stained-glass
windows (pictured, p100). Most of it was built in
1448, but two arches in the chancel date back
to around 1200. Carved 15th-century ceiling
bosses in its hexagonal porch include a sheep
overpowering a wolf, and the possibly pagan
but common visitor to British churches, the
Green Man – look for his leafy beard.

Chipping Norton Museum

Squeezed into the upper floor of a little house
facing the imposing columns of the town hall,
Chipping Norton's volunteer-run **museum**
(☏01608-641712; www.chippingnortonmuseum.org.
uk; 4 High St; £1.50; ⊙2-4pm Mon-Sat Easter-Oct)
is a small-scale and resolutely local affair, using
assorted mannequins and memorabilia to tell
the Chippy story.

Bliss Tweed Mill

Chipping Norton's most striking landmark, the
1872 Bliss Tweed Mill dominates its western
outskirts. Looking much more like a stately
home than a factory, it's topped by a dome
from which a towering chimney, designed to
resemble a Tuscan column, emerges in turn.
After the mill ceased production in 1980 it was
converted into flats, so content yourself with
admiring it from the A44 as you drive past.

Nearby: Chastleton House

Built between 1607 and 1612 and barely altered
since, **Chastleton House** (pictured; Map p102,
D3; NT; ☏01608-674355; www.nationaltrust.org.uk/
chastle ton-house; Chastleton; adult/child £9.50/5;
⊙1-5pm Wed-Sun Mar-Oct; P) is one of England's

✕ Take a Break

Wild Thyme (www.
wildthymerestaurant.
co.uk; 10 New St;
2/3-course dinner
£32/40; ⊙7-9pm Tue
& Wed, noon-2pm &
7-9pm Thu, noon-2pm
& 6.30-9.30pm Fri &
Sat) thrills palates
with top-notch crea-
tive dishes.

**Jaffé & Neale
Bookshop Cafe**
(www.jaffeandneale.
co.uk; 1 Middle Row;
⊙9.30am-5.30pm
Mon-Fri, 9am-5.30pm
Sat, 11am-5pm Sun;
☏) is a cosy little
cafe in a busy inde-
pendent bookshop.

Producat terra animam viventem in genere suo

The Chipping Norton Set

Chipping Norton is best known in Britain as the epicentre of the so-called 'Chipping Norton set', an amorphous but generally conservative group of political/media movers and shakers that includes former prime minister (and former local MP) David Cameron and Top Gear presenter Jeremy Clarkson. They live and socialise in the surrounding villages, though, so Chipping Norton itself doesn't really have the chi-chi restaurants and exclusive hotels you might expect. Its major annual get-together is the **Big Feastival** (www.thebigfeastival.com; Churchill Heath Farm, Kingman; day tickets £64, weekend camping tickets £179.50; ⏱late Aug; 👪), combining food and music on the farm of Blur bassist Alex James.

finest and most complete Jacobean houses. Five miles northwest of Chipping Norton, signposted off the A44 halfway to Moreton-in-Marsh, it's bursting with rare tapestries, family portraits and antique furniture; the Long Gallery is particularly resplendent. Outside, there's a wonderful topiary garden. Free garden tours run most afternoons.

Nearby: Rollright Stones

Linked by a footpath through open fields, the ancient **Rollright Stones** (Map p102, E2; www.rollright stones.co.uk; off A3400, Great Rollright; suggested donation £1; ⏱24hr) stand to either side of an unnamed road 4 miles north of Chipping Norton. The most remarkable, the King's Men, consist of the weathered remnants of a stone circle that surrounded a Neolithic ceremonial centre in around 2500 BC, while the taller King Stone probably marked a Bronze Age cemetery, a millennium later.

Nearby: Cotswolds Distillery

This ambitious, ecofriendly gin and whisky **distillery** (Map p102, E1; ☎01608-238533; www.cotswoldsdistillery.com; Phillip's Field, Whichford Rd, Stourton; tours with/without tasting £10/6; ⏱tours 11am, 1pm & 3pm, shop 9am-5pm Mon-Sat, 11am-4pm Sun) sits tucked into the northern Cotswolds, 8 miles north of Chipping Norton. Join a tour of the facilities to learn how its delicious Cotswolds-flavoured liquors are produced, then wrap things up with a tasting session. Reservations essential.

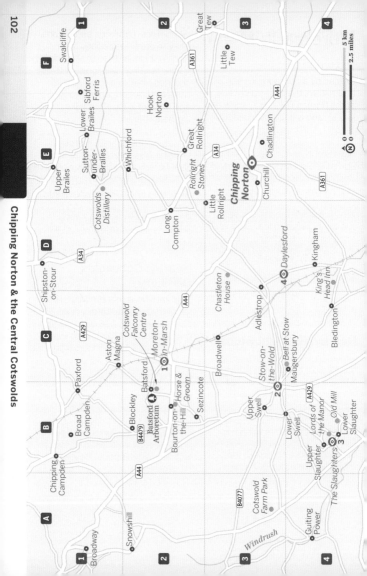

Swalcliffe

Great Tew

Little Tew

Sibford Ferris

Lower Braies

Hook Norton

Upper Braies

Sutton-under-Braies

Whichford

Great Rollright

Chadlington

Cotswolds Distillery

Rollright Stones

Little Rollright

Chipping Norton

Churchill

Shipston-on-Stour

Long Compton

Kingham

King's Head Inn

Paxford

Aston Magna

Cotswold Falconry Centre

Moreton-in-Marsh 1

Chastleton House

Adlestrop

Daylesford 4

Biedington

Broad Campden

Blockley

Batsford

Batsford Arboretum

Bourton-on-the-Hill

Sezincote

Broadwell

Stow-on-the-Wold

Bell at Stow

Maugersbury

2

Chipping Campden

Upper Swell

Lower Swell

Lords of the Manor

Old Mill

Lower Slaughter

3

Broadway

Snowshill

Upper Slaughter

The Slaughters

Cotswold Farm Park

Guiting Power

Windrush

N

5 km

2.5 miles

Moreton-in-Marsh

1 ⊙ MAP 102, C2

Graced by an ultrabroad High St that follows the die-straight line of the Roman Fosse Way (now the A429), and is lined with beautiful 17th- and 18th-century buildings, the historic Cotswolds town of Moreton-in-Marsh stands 8 miles northwest of Chipping Norton. Sadly it's rather marred by constant heavy traffic, but take the time to wander around – ideally on a Tuesday, when the weekly market bursts into life – and you'll find plenty of tearooms, cafes and pubs, along with intriguing shops.

Created from 1880 onwards by Bertie Mitford (Lord Redesdale), and later briefly home to his famous granddaughters, the Mitford sisters, the exotic 22-hectare **Batsford Arboretum** (Map p102, B2; ☑01386-701441; www.batsarb. co.uk; Batsford Park; adult/child £7.95/3.30; ☉9am-5pm Mon-Sat, from 10am Sun), 1.5 miles west of Moreton, holds rare or endangered trees, bamboos and shrubs. They're drawn especially from Nepal, China and Japan, with highlights including flowering Japanese cherries (at their best in spring), vast North American redwoods, and the strangely churchlike 'cathedral' lime.

In a tiny hamlet 2 miles west of Moreton-in-Marsh, **Horse & Groom** (Map p102, B2; ☑01386-700413; www.horseandgroom.info; A44, Bourton-on-the-Hill; mains £12-23; ☉noon-3pm & 6.30-9.30pm Mon-Sat, to 8.30pm Sun; P🛜) is a laid-back but welcoming pub, a firm favourite with well-heeled types who appreciate its array of gins. As well as serving good food, it also has five swish rooms upstairs.

In an appealing historic cottage on the main road, **Martha's Coffee House** (Gavel Cottage, High St; mains £7-9; ☉9am-5pm Mon-Sat, to 4pm Sun; 🛜♿) serves all-day breakfasts, cream teas, sandwiches and savoury scones.

The Flight of the Falcons

The **Cotswold Falconry Centre** (Map p102, B2; ☑01386-701043; www. cotswold-falconry.co.uk; Batsford Park; adult/child £10/5; ☉10.30am-5pm mid-Feb–mid-Nov; P), 2 miles west of Moreton-in-Marsh, is home to over 150 birds of prey, including owls, vultures and eagles as well, of course, as falcons. It stages thrilling displays of the ancient practice of falconry, at 11.30am, 1.30pm and 3pm daily, with an additional 4.30pm show between April and October. Hands-on experiences (from £40) include a one-hour 'Flying Start' during which visitors get to fly hawks. The birds fly best on windy days.

Stow-on-the-Wold

2 ⊙ MAP 102, B3

The Cotswolds' highest town, Stow-on-the-Wold stands at the junction of six roads 9 miles west of Chipping Norton and 4.5 miles south of Moreton-in-Marsh. The high-walled alleyways that lead into its large central square originally served to funnel sheep into the fair. Surrounded by handsome buildings, the square witnessed a bloody massacre at the end of the English Civil War, when Roundhead soldiers dispatched defeated Royalists in 1646. Still an important market town, Stow is also a major tourist destination, packed with visitors in summer, and famous for hosting the twice-yearly **Stow Horse Fair** (⊙mid-May & late Oct).

The **Cotswold Farm Park** (Map p102, A3; ☎01451-850307; www.cotswoldfarmpark.co.uk; Guiting Power; adult/child £14/12.50; ⊙10.30am-5pm mid-Feb–late Dec; P🚼), 6 miles west, sets out to introduce children to the world of farm animals, while preserving rare breeds such as Exmoor ponies and Cotswold Lion sheep. It offers milking demonstrations, lamb-feeding sessions, an adventure playground, pedal tractors to ride on, and a 2-mile wildlife walk.

Among the best of Stow's lively old pubs, the **Bell at Stow** (Map p102, C4; ☎01451-870916; www.thebellatstow.com; Park St; mains £14-25; ⊙food served noon-9.30pm; 🚼) lurks on the eastern edge of town, covered in greenery. Its enticing menu stretches from burgers and steaks to couscous-stuffed peppers and cheese boards, with daily fish and seafood specials.

'Pub of the Year' in 2018, and set in a 16th-century cider house with a lovely garden 4 miles southeast of Stow, the **King's Head Inn** (Map p102, D4; ☎01608-658365; www.thekingsheadinn.net; The Green, Bledington; mains £14-25.50; ⊙noon-2pm & 6.30-9pm Mon-Sat, to 9.30pm Fri & Sat, noon-3pm & 6.30-9pm Sun; P🚲) is ideal for eating, drinking or both. Seasonal menus draw on local produce such as Cotswold lamb, adding Mediterranean flavours (mozzarella and pomegranate salad), while hearty £8 to £10 sandwiches or cheese platters make a satisfying lunch.

The Slaughters

3 ⊙ MAP 102, B4

Despite their many visitors, the picture-postcard villages of Upper and Lower Slaughter, around 3.5 miles southwest of Stow-on-the-Wold, have somehow managed to maintain their unhurried medieval charm. Their names have nothing to do with abattoirs; they come from the Old English *'sloughtre,'* meaning slough or muddy place.

Meandering through the two villages, the River Eye passes a succession of classic gold-tinged Cotswolds houses. Lower Slaughter is the real gem, with the river flowing just inches below road level, and flowery footpaths to either side.

Lower Slaughter

Right on the river, the **Old Mill** (Map p102, B4; 01451-820052; www.oldmill-lowerslaughter.com; Lower Slaughter; adult/child £2.50/1; 10am-6pm Mar-Oct, to dusk Nov-Feb) houses a cafe, a crafts shop and a small museum. A watermill is recorded as operating in this location as far back as the Domesday Book (1086).

Set inside a dazzling countryside manor, **Lords of the Manor** (Map p102, B4; 01451-820243; www.lordsofthemanor.com; Upper Slaughter; 3-/7-course dinner £72.50/£90; noon-1.30pm Sat & Sun, 6.45-9pm daily; P) is a romantic restaurant – be sure to book ahead – that concocts beautifully presented dishes with French touches and plenty of quality local produce. It also serves popular afternoon teas. On weekdays lunch is available in the bar only.

Daylesford

4 MAP 102, D3

A country-chic temple to the Cotswolds' organic movement, 4 miles east of Stow, the sprawling **Daylesford Organic** (01608-731700; www.daylesford.com; Daylesford; 8am-8pm Mon-Sat, 10am-4pm Sun) was kickstarted 40 years ago when a family farm turned sustainable. Centring on a gleaming food hall, crammed with Daylesford-brand produce, it also holds an excellent cafe-restaurant serving organic-fuelled treats (£13 to £19), plus an upmarket boutique, rental cottages, and luxury spa.

Explore ✦

Chipping Campden

A standout gem, even in a region that's renowned for its pretty towns, Chipping Campden is a glorious reminder of Cotswolds life in medieval times. While 'Chipping' derives from the Old English 'ceapen', meaning 'market', it owes its conspicuous prosperity – and its beautiful honey-coloured buildings – to its success in the wool trade.

Chipping Campden's gracefully curving main street is flanked by a picturesque array of stone cottages, ancient inns and historic homes, with Market Hall (p109) and Grevel House (p109) as the pick of the bunch. Spend a day here to have time to see St James' Church (p109) and the Court Barn Museum (p110), and head out to the Arts and Crafts garden at nearby Hidcote (p110). Feed your engines with afternoon tea at Badgers Hall (p111), and a good meal at the Eight Bells (p111).

Getting There & Around

🚗 To reach Chipping Campden, leave the A44 4 miles southeast of Broadway, and head 2.5 miles northeast on the B4081. Parking is very hard to find, year-round.

🚌 Johnsons Excel routes 1 and 2 connect with Moreton-in-Marsh (£3.90, 50 minutes), Broadway (£2.90, 20 minutes) and Stratford (£4.40, 50 minutes). Marchants buses 606 and 606S serve Broadway (£2.90, 20 minutes), Stratford (£4.80, 25 minutes) and Winchcombe (£5.60, 35 minutes).

St James' Church

Sights

St James' Church

Built in Perpendicular Gothic style in the late 15th century using wool-trade profits, this imposing church boasts a splendid tower and some graceful 17th-century monuments. One of the earliest priest vestments on record, dating back to around 1400, is screened behind a curtain inside. The remarkable row of almshouses along Church St a short walk south was constructed in 1612. (📞01386-841927; www.stjameschurchcampden.co.uk; Church St; admission free; 🕙11am-4pm Mon-Sat, noon-4pm Sun Apr-Sep, to 3pm Oct-Mar)

Market Hall

Chipping Campden's highly photogenic, honey-toned, little 17th-century Market Hall, an open-sided pillared building where dairy farmers used to sell their produce, stands halfway along the high street. With its simple arches, lumpy stone floors, multiple gables and elaborate timber roof, it looks like a cross between a barn and a chapel. (NT; www.nationaltrust.org.uk/market-hall; High St; admission free; 🕙24hr)

Grevel House

Built around 1380 for the supremely prosperous wool merchant William Grevel, complete with gargoyles and mullioned windows, Grevel House is Chipping Campden's oldest building. It's

Market Hall

PETER NADOLSKI / SHUTTERSTOCK ©

Walking & Cycling from Chipping Campden

As the northeastern end of the Cotswold Way, a long-distance path that rambles for 102 miles southwest all the way to Bath, Chipping Campden is a major rendezvous for Cotswolds walkers and cyclists.

Cotswold Country Cycles (☎01386-438706; www.cotswoldcountry cycles.com; Longlands Farm Cottage; 3 day/2 night tours from £285), based just outside the village, organises maps, luggage transfers and B&B stays for self-guided cycling tours of varying lengths and degrees of difficulty.

still a private home, but you can admire its splendid Perpendicular Gothic–style gabled window and sundial from the street. (High St; ⊙closed to the public)

Court Barn Museum

Ever since architect and designer Charles Robert Ashbee (1863–1942) moved his Guild of Handicraft here from east London in 1902, Chipping Campden has been linked with the Arts and Crafts movement. This small but interesting museum displays work by nine luminaries of the movement, which celebrated traditional artisans in an age of industrialisation. Sadly, robberies in 2011 and 2017 removed its prize jewellery collection, but surviving artefacts include sculpture, book-binding and ceramics. It also stages two selling exhibitions each year. (☎01386-841951; www.courtbarn. org.uk; Church St; adult/child £5/free; ⊙10am-5pm Tue-Sun Apr-Sep, to 4pm Oct-Mar)

Old Silk Mill

This former silk mill (c 1790) was the home of Charles Robert Ashbee's Guild of Handicraft from 1902 until it went bust in 1908. Many artisans stayed on, however. Hart Gold & Silversmiths are still here today, along with assorted woodturners, ceramicists, metalworkers and the like, and the **Gallery at the Guild** sells their work. (☎01386-840345; www. thegalleryattheguild.co.uk; Sheep St; admission free; ⊙10am-5pm Apr-Oct, 10am-4.30pm Mon-Thu, to 5pm Fri & Sat, Nov-Mar)

Hidcote

Hidcote, 4 miles northeast of Chipping Campden, ranks among the finest Arts and Crafts gardens in Britain. Laid out from 1907 onwards by American horticulturalist Lawrence Johnston, and acquired by the National Trust in 1948, it consists of a series of outdoor 'rooms' filled with flowers and rare plants from across the globe. There's also a cafe and garden centre. (NT; www.nationaltrust.org.uk/

Badgers Hall

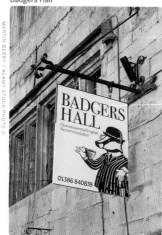

MARTIN BERRY / ALAMY STOCK PHOTO ©

BADGERS HALL

Quintessential English Accommodation

01386 840839

hidcote; Hidcote Bartrim; adult/child £10.90/5.45; ⏱10am-6pm Apr-Sep, to 5pm Oct, shorter hours Nov, Dec & mid-Feb–Mar, closed Jan; P)

Eating

Badgers Hall   BAKERY £

Set in a glorious old mansion facing the market hall, this definitive Cotswold tearoom is renowned for its no-holds-barred afternoon teas, served from 2.30pm onwards. Lunch is also a treat, starring the most wonderful cheese scones you've ever tasted. Guests staying in the cosy B&B rooms upstairs (£140) get to sample its baking all week; nonguests are welcome Thursday to Saturday only. (☎01386-840839; www.badgershall. com; High St; lunch mains £6-12,

afternoon tea per person £6.50-25; ⏱8am-5.30pm Thu-Sat; ✍)

Eight Bells Inn   PUB FOOD ££

Nestled into a delightfully updated 14th-century inn, this relaxed pub wins points for its flagstone floors, warm service and good modern-British country cooking. Options range from beer-battered cod to braised lamb shank or goat's-cheese tagliatelle, plus chunky sandwiches for lunch. Upstairs, there are smart, characterful rooms. (☎01386-840371; www. eightbellsinn.co.uk; Church St; mains £13-23; ⏱noon-2pm & 6.30-9pm Mon-Thu, noon-2.30pm & 6.30-9.30pm Fri & Sat, noon-3pm & 6-8.30pm Sun; ♿🐾)

Campden Coffee Company   CAFE £

It's a shame about the generic-sounding name, because this is actually a very pleasant cafe, peacefully located in the historic Old Silk Mill, with nice courtyard seating as well as a bright, large main room. In addition to baked goods – also prominent at breakfast – the wholesome lunch menu includes soup, salads and daily specials. The coffee's good, too. (☎01386-849251; www.facebook.com/campden-coffee; Old Silk Mill, Sheep St; mains £5-8; ⏱9.45am-3.50pm Mon, 8.45am-3.50pm Tue-Fri, 9.45am-4.15pm Sat & Sun; 📶✍♿)

Worth a Trip 📷
Stratford-upon-Avon

Author of many of the most quoted lines in the English language, William Shakespeare was born in the oh-so-Tudor town of Stratford-upon-Avon, 40 miles northwest of Oxford, and died here in 1616. Pay your respects at his modest grave, catch a performance by the Royal Shakespeare Company and treat yourself to a cream tea in a Bard-themed tearoom.

Town car parks charge high fees, 24 hours a day.

A hand-wound chain **ferry** (10am-6pm Apr-Oct) crosses the Avon between the west bank and the east bank.

A bicycle is handy for getting out to the outlying Shakespeare properties.

Shakespeare's Birthplace

Exhibits in **Shakespeare's Birthplace** (☏01789-204016; www.shakespeare.org.uk; Henley St; adult/child £17.50/11.50; ⊙9am-5pm Apr-Aug, to 4.30pm Sep & Oct, 10am-3.30pm Nov-Mar), where he was born in 1564, include restored Tudor rooms.

Shakespeare's New Place

When Shakespeare retired, he swapped the bright lights of London for **New Place** (☏01789-338536; www.shakespeare.org.uk; cnr Chapel St & Chapel Lane; adult/child £12.50/8; ⊙10am-5pm Apr-Aug, to 4.30pm Sep & Oct, to 3.30pm Nov-Feb), where he died in 1616. Displays help to bring the long-demolished town house to life.

Anne Hathaway's Cottage

Childhood home to Shakespeare's future bride, the delightful **Anne Hathaway's Cottage** (☏01789-338532; www.shakespeare.org.uk; Cottage Lane, Shottery; adult/child £12.50/8; ⊙9am-5pm Apr-Aug, to 4.30pm Sep & Oct, 10am-3.30pm Nov-Mar) stands 1 mile west of Stratford. It has period furniture, gorgeous gardens and an arboretum holding every tree mentioned in Shakespeare's plays.

Royal Shakespeare Company

Book well in advance for performances by the renowned **RSC** (RSC; ☏box office 01789-403493; www.rsc.org.uk; Waterside; tours adult £7-9, child £4.50-5, tower adult/child £2.50/1.25; ⊙tour times vary, tower 10am-5pm Sun-Fri, 10am-12.15pm & 2-5pm Sat mid-Mar–mid-Oct, 10am-4.30pm Sun-Fri, to 12.15pm Sat mid-Oct–mid-Mar), in the Royal Shakespeare Theatre or Swan Theatre. A few tickets are sold on the actual day.

★ The Full Story

All sites listed here are run by the Shakespeare Birthplace Trust (www.shakespeare.org.uk), and sell and accept the Full Story ticket (adult/child £22/14.50), also available online.

✕ Take A Break

Stratford is bursting with high-quality eating and drinking options, including **Salt** (☏01789-263566; www.salt-restaurant.co.uk; 8 Church St; 2-/3-course menus lunch £33.50/37, dinner £37/45; ⊙noon-2pm & 6.30-10pm Wed-Sat, noon-2pm Sun), an intimate bistro, and the **Old Thatch Tavern** (www.oldthatchtavernstratford.co.uk; Greenhill St; ⊙11.30am-11pm Mon-Sat, from noon Sun; ⊛), a thatched-roofed pub dating back to 1470.

Explore

Broadway & the Northwest Cotswolds

The quintessentially English village of Broadway, just 5 miles west of Chipping Campden, has long been one of the Cotswolds' most popular destinations. During the Victorian era it attracted the likes of writer-designer William Morris and artist John Singer Sargent. Its graceful, golden-hued cottages, set at the foot of a steep escarpment, now hold antique shops, tearooms and art galleries, interspersed with luxurious hotels.

Allow half a day to explore Broadway itself and see the fine art in the Broadway Museum (p117), pausing for a meal in 5 North St (p123) and a drink in the Crown & Trumpet (p117). Then visit hilltop Broadway Tower (p117) before continuing to the ancient market town of Winchcombe (p121), 8 miles south, where superb Sudeley Castle played a prominent role in Tudor history.

Getting There & Around

🚌 Marchants and Johnsons ExcelBus services head to Cheltenham (route 606/606S; £3.20, 40 minutes), Chipping Campden (route 1/2/606S; £2.90, 20 minutes), Moreton-in-Marsh (route 1/2; £3.90, 30 minutes), Stratford-upon-Avon (route 1/2/24/606S; £4.40, 45 minutes) and Winchcombe (route 606/606S; £3, 30 minutes).

Broadway & the Northwest Cotswolds Map on p120

Broadway Tower (p117) ROSANEMILLER PHOTOGRAPHY / GETTY IMAGES ©

Top Sights 📷
Broadway

The graceful, golden-hued cottages of the quin-tessentially English village of Broadway, set at the foot of a steep escarpment, now hold antique shops, tearooms and art galleries, interspersed with luxurious hotels. The village was a magnet for artists from the Arts and Crafts movement in the 19th and early 20th centuries, and is still a centre for the arts today.

◉ MAP P120, D1

By car, the main approach road to Broadway is the A44, which connects Oxford to Worcester.

Broadway Museum & Art Gallery

Set in a magnificent 17th-century coaching inn, Broadway's town **museum** (📞01386-859047; www.ashmoleanbroadway.org; Tudor House, 65 High St; adult/child £5/2; ⏰10am-5pm Tue-Sun Feb-Oct, to 4pm Nov & Dec, closed Jan) has close links with Oxford's prestigious Ashmolean Museum. Its fascinating displays of local crafts, art and antiques, and its stimulating temporary exhibitions, draw exclusively on the Ashmolean collection, so the quality is consistently high. Paintings in the sumptuous upstairs galleries include 18th-century works by Joshua Reynolds and Thomas Gainsborough.

Nearby: Snowshill Manor & Garden

Once home to eccentric poet and architect Charles Paget Wade (1883–1956), this wonderful medieval **mansion** (Map p120, D2; NT; www.nationaltrust.org.uk; Snowshill; adult/child £12.80/6.40; ⏰noon-5pm mid-Mar–Oct, 11am-2.30pm Sat & Sun Nov) stands just over 2 miles south of Broadway. It now displays Wade's extraordinary collection of crafts and design, ranging from musical instruments to Southeast Asian masks and Japanese samurai armour.

Nearby: Broadway Tower

Built in 1798 to resemble an imaginary Saxon fort, the **Broadway Tower** (Map p120, D1; 📞01386-852390; www.broadwaytower.co.uk; Middle Hill; adult/child £5/3, with Cold War Experience £8.50/5; ⏰10am-5pm; P) is a turreted Gothic folly looking down on Broadway from atop the escarpment, 1 mile southeast. William Morris spent a summer here, so exhibitions on its successive levels focus on the Arts and Crafts movement. The main reason to visit, though, is for the stunning all-round views from its rooftop platform.

✕ Take a Break

Broadway Deli (pictured; www.broadwaydeli.co.uk; 29 High St; dishes £5-10; ⏰8am-5pm Mon-Sat, 9am-3pm Sun; 🖉) If it's not sunny enough to eat in this buzzing deli's garden, head up the creaky stairs to find red-clothed indoor tables instead. Either way, you can enjoy charcuterie platters, chunky sandwiches, and steaming bowls of soup.

Crown & Trumpet (www.cotswoldholidays.co.uk; 14 Church St; ⏰11am-11pm; 📶) is much the nicest of Broadway's pubs. Its cosy bar and front garden filled at the weekend with lively locals, the Crown & Trumpet has been honoured by CAMRA (the Campaign for Real Ale) for its carefully kept, seasonally varying array of fine beers. There's also good pub grub, and frequent live music.

Return of the Railway

Rail service returned to Broadway in 2018 after a 58-year hiatus, with the reopening of the long-defunct **Broadway Station**, just under a mile northwest of town. Most days in summer, following an intricate schedule, the volunteer-run **Gloucestershire Warwickshire Railway** (pictured, left; GWR; Map p120, A4; ☏01242-621405; www.gwsr.com; day pass adult/child £18/8; ⊙Mar-Dec; ☺) runs around five excursion trains – many of them steam-powered, the rest 'heritage diesel' – between Cheltenham racecourse and Broadway, via Winchcombe, for a return fare of £18.

Nearby: Cold War Experience

A long-buried secret lies a minute's walk north of Broadway Tower, in the cramped cellar-like form of a **bunker** (Map p120, D1; ☏01386-852390; www.broadwaytower.co.uk; Broadway Tower, Middle Hill; adult/child £8.50/5; ⊙10am-4pm Sat & Sun Apr-Oct; ℗) where, until 1991, members of the Royal Observer Corps watched out for nuclear attacks. On summer weekends, regular tour groups descend its steep access ladder to find themselves in a tiny room holding astonishingly low-tech devices like the 'Bomb Power Indicator'.

Nearby: St Eadburgha's Church

It's well worth taking the time to wander down to lovely 12th-century **St Eadburgha's Church** (Map p120, D1; www.stmichaelsbroad-way.org; Snowshill Rd; admission free; ⊙10am-dusk), a signposted 1-mile walk south of Broadway.

Nearby: Stanway House

There's little more to the pretty village of Stanway, 5 miles southwest of Broadway towards Winchcombe. than a few thatch-roofed cottages, a church and this magnificent Jacobean **mansion** (Map p120, C2; ☏01386-584469; www.stanwayfountain.co.uk; Stanway; adult/child £9/4; ⊙2-5pm Tue & Thu Jun-Aug), concealed behind a triple-gabled gatehouse. Its beautiful baroque water gardens feature Britain's tallest fountain, which erupts, geyser-like, to 300ft. The private home of the Earls of Wemyss for 500 years, the manor has a delightful, lived-in charm, with much of its original furniture and character intact.

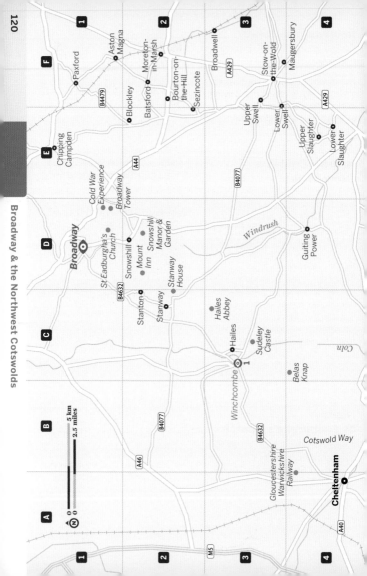

A **B** **C** **D** **E** **F**

1 **2** **3** **4**

5 km
2.5 miles

N

Paxford
Aston Magna
Blockley
Batsford
Moreton-in-Marsh
Bourton-on-the-Hill
Sezincote
Broadwell
Stow-on-the-Wold
Maugersbury
A429
A429
Chipping Campden
Upper Swell
Lower Swell
Cold War Experience
Broadway Tower
A44
Upper Slaughter
Lower Slaughter
Broadway
St Eadburgha's Church
B4632
Snowshill
Mount Inn
Snowshill Manor & Garden
Stanway House
B4077
Windrush
Guiting Power
Stanton
Stanway
Hailes Abbey
Hailes
A46
B4077
Sudeley Castle
Coln
Belas Knap
Winchcombe
B4632
Gloucestershire Warwickshire Railway
Cotswold Way
Cheltenham
A40
M5

Winchcombe

1 MAP 120, C3

Winchcombe, 8 miles southwest of Broadway, is very much a living, working town, where butchers, bakers and independent shops line the main streets. Capital of the Anglo-Saxon kingdom of Mercia, it remained a major trading town until the Middle Ages, and was a centre for (illegally) growing tobacco in the 17th century. Of its dramatic stone and half-timbered buildings, the much-restored, 15th-century Perpendicular **St Peter's Church** (www.winchcombeparish.org.uk; Gloucester St; 8.30am-5.30pm Apr-Oct, to 4pm Nov-Mar) is worth a visit for its majestic tower, arcaded interior and grotesque gargoyles.

Mount Inn

Revelling in glorious hilltop views above pretty honey-washed Stanton, just off the Cotswolds Way 3.5 miles southwest of Broadway, the **Mount Inn** (Map p120, D2; 01386-584316; www.themountinn.co.uk; Stanton; mains £13-22; noon-2pm & 6-9pm Mon-Sat, to 8pm Sun; P) is not only idyllically located, but also serves great food: hearty country favourites, prepared with contemporary flair. Menus range over breaded local St Eadburgha cheese, beer-battered haddock, gammon steaks, mushroom-halloumi burgers and seasonal specials.

Street scene, Winchcombe

Walkers approaching Broadway

In a stunning hilltop location south of Winchcombe, and best accessed via a 2.5-mile hike on the Cotswold Way, **Belas Knap Long Barrow** (EH; Map p120, C4; www.english-heritage.org.uk; near Charlton Abbots; admission free; ☉dawn-dusk) is one of the country's best-preserved neolithic burial chambers, dating from around 3000 BC.

Now lying in ruins 3 miles northeast of Winchcombe, 13th-century **Hailes Abbey** (EH; Map p120, C3; www.english-heritage.org.uk; Hailes; adult/child £5.90/3.50; ☉10am-6pm Jul & Aug, to 5pm Easter-Jun, Sep & Oct; ℗) was once an important pilgrimage centre, mentioned in

Sudeley Castle

During its thousand-year history, **Sudeley Castle** (Map p120, C3; ☎01242-604244; www.sudeleycastle.co.uk; adult/child £16.50/7.50; ☉10am-5pm mid-Mar–Oct; ℗ ♿), half a mile southeast of Winchcombe, has welcomed monarchs including Richard III, Henry VIII and Charles I. It's most famous as the home and final resting place of Catherine Parr, widow of Henry VIII, who lived here with her fourth husband, Thomas Seymour. This is the only private house in England where a queen is buried – Catherine lies in its Perpendicular Gothic St Mary's Church.

Henry VIII and Anne Boleyn visited Sudeley together in 1535. Anne's daughter, Princess Elizabeth – later to become Elizabeth I – was part of the household until Seymour's inappropriate displays of affection prompted Catherine to send her away. Lady Jane Grey (the ill-fated 'Nine Days Queen') also lived here, and was chief mourner at Catherine's 1548 funeral.

Self-guided tours lead through the house, which is still a family home. The 10 separate gardens in the gorgeous grounds include spectacular avenues of sculpted yews, an intricate knot garden, and aviaries containing colourful pheasants. Four Tudor queens – Anne Boleyn, Catherine Parr, Lady Jane Grey and Elizabeth I – strolled through the rose-filled Queens' Garden.

Walks from Winchcombe

Winchcombe makes a superb base for walkers. Long-distance trails branch out in every direction, including the 102-mile Cotswold Way, the Gloucestershire Way (which tracks 100 miles from Chepstow to Tewkesbury) and the 55-mile, Worcestershire-bound St Kenelm's Way.

Plenty of shorter walks also set off from Winchcombe, such as a 5.5-mile loop trail that takes in Belas Knap Long Barrow and Sudeley Castle.

Winchcombe Welcomes Walkers (www.winchcombewelcomes walkers.com) has good walking information, along with download-able itineraries and maps, and organises the three-day Winchcombe Cotswold Walking Festival in mid-May.

Chaucer's *Canterbury Tales* as possessing a vial of Christ's blood.

The veteran **5 North St** (☎01242-604566; www.5northstreetrestaurant.co.uk; 5 North St; 2-/3-course lunch £26/32, 3-/7-course dinner £54/74; ☉7-9pm Tue, 12.30-1.30pm & 7-9pm Wed-Sat, 12.30-1.30pm Sun; 🚮) gourmet restaurant is a treat from start to finish, from its splendid 400-year-old timbered exterior to the elegant, inventive creations you eventually find on your plate. Marcus Ashenford's cooking is rooted in traditional seasonal ingredients, but the odd playful experiment (think duck-egg pasta or malt ice cream) adds that extra magic. Vegetarians can enjoy a separate £40 menu.

Explore

Burford & the Southeast Cotswolds

Gliding down a steep hillside to an ancient river crossing, 20 miles west of Oxford, Burford has hardly changed since its medieval glory days. Small and very picturesque, it holds an appealing mix of stone cottages, gold-tinged town houses, antique shops, chintzy tearooms and delightful hotels and restaurants.

After seeing Burford's wonderfully preserved church (p127), enjoy a good meal at Huffkins (p127) or the Angel (p127). Sleepy Northleach just west also boasts a great inn, the Wheatsheaf (p129), with the impressive Chedworth Roman Villa (p130) in the countryside nearby. South of Burford, tiny Bibury (p130), home to lovely Arlington Row, was hailed as 'England's most beautiful village' by William Morris, who lived in Kelmscott Manor.

Getting There & Around

🚌 Stagecoach and Swanbrook buses connect Burford with Oxford (route 853; £6.30, 45 minutes to 1¼ hours), Northleach (route 853; £2.40, 15 minutes), Minster Lovell (route 233/853; £2.30, 15 minutes), Woodstock (route 233; £4.10, 45 minutes) and Cheltenham (route 853; £4.50, 45 minutes).

Burford & the Southeast Cotswolds Map on p128

Arlington Row, Burford (p126) JOHN SPREADBURY / SHUTTERSTOCK ©

Top Sights 📷
Burford

Locals insist it's a town not a village, having received its charter in 1090, but it's a very small town, and a very picturesque one too. A wonderfully preserved, centuries-old church and an array of delightful hotels and restaurants make Burford an attractive stop. Antique shops, chintzy tearooms and specialist boutiques peddle nostalgia to summer visitors, but it's easy to escape the crowds.

◉ MAP P128, D1

Standing conveniently just north of the A40, Burford is one of the easiest Cotswold towns to reach by road. It's often the first port of call for drivers coming from Oxford (20 miles east) or London (75 miles southeast).

St John the Baptist's Church

Burford's splendid **church** (pictured; www.burford church.org; Church Lane; ⏱9am-5pm), near the river, took over three centuries to build, from 1175 onwards. Its fan-vaulted ceiling, Norman west doorway and 15th-century spire remain intact. The star attraction is the macabre 1625 Tanfield tomb, depicting local nobleman Sir Lawrence Tanfield and his wife lying in finery above a pair of carved skeletons, one leg bone of which is said to be real.

Tolsey Museum

This engaging local **museum** (📞01993-822178; www.tolseymuseumburford.org; cnr High & Sheep Sts; admission free; ⏱2-5pm Tue-Sun, closed Nov-Mar) occupies the upper floor of an unusual 16th-century building with a columned open arcade at street level, where traders once paid their market tolls. The museum itself covers Burford's historical crafts and industries, by which people have made everything from clocks and clarinets to dolls' houses and metallic mortars.

Nearby: Cotswold Wildlife Park

Younger visitors will enjoy this hugely popular **wildlife centre** (Map p128, D2; 📞01993-823006; www.cotswoldwildlifepark.co.uk; Bradwell Grove; adult/child £16/10.50; ⏱10am-6pm Apr-Oct, to 5pm or dusk Nov-Mar, last admission 2hr before closing), 3 miles south of Burford. Its vast menagerie includes penguins, zebras, lions, reindeer, anacondas, endangered white rhinos and a giant tortoise. A miniature train adds to the excitement.

Nearby: St Mary's Church

This 12th-century **church** (Map p128, E1; ⏱10am-dusk) in Swinbrook, 3 miles east of Burford, is remarkable for the tomb of the Fettiplace family, who dominated this area for 500 years. Several members of a more recent prominent family, the Mitford sisters, are also buried here.

✕ Take a Break

Angel (www.theangel atburford.co.uk; 14 Witney St; mains £14-25; ⏱noon-9.30pm; 📶🅿♿🐾) is set in a stylishly revamped 16th-century inn, with roaring fires and cosy booths.

Huffkins (www. huffkins.com; 98 High St; mains £6-15; ⏱9am-4.30pm Mon-Fri, to 5pm Sat, 10am-5pm Sun) bakes delicious scones, cakes and pies.

Spice Lounge (www. spiceloungeburford. co.uk; 81 High St; mains £9-16; ⏱noon-2pm & 6-10pm Sat-Thu, 6-10pm Fri; ✒) has excellent Bangladeshi and Indian food.

Lamb Inn (www. cotswold-inns-hotels. co.uk/the-lamb-inn; Sheep St; mains £14-35; ⏱7.30-10am, noon-2.30pm & 7-9pm) does modern British cuisine, with an especially good grill menu.

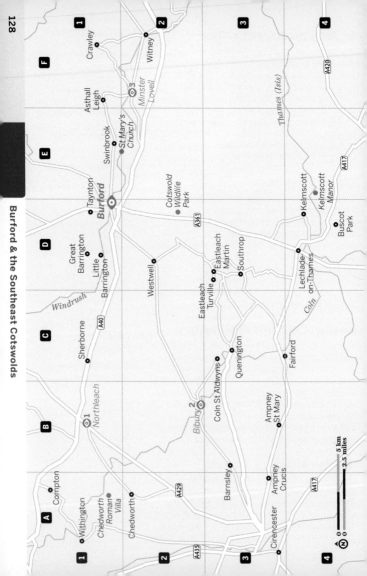

Burford & the Southeast Cotswolds

F
Crawley
Witney

E
Asthall
Leigh
Minster Lovell
Swinbrook
St Mary's Church
Taynton
Burford
Cotswold Wildlife Park
A361
Kelmscott
Kelmscott Manor
Buscot Park
A417
Thames (Isis)
A420

D
Great Barrington
Little Barrington
Westwell
Eastleach Martin
Eastleach Turville
Southrop
Lechlade-on-Thames
Coln
Fairford

C
Sherborne
A40
Windrush
Quenington
Coln St Aldwyns
Bibury
Northleach

B
Compton
Chedworth Roman Villa
Chedworth
A429
Barnsley
Ampney St Mary
Ampney Crucis
A417

A
Withington

Cirencester
A433
A435

5 km
2.5 miles
0
0
N

1 **2** **3** **4**

Northleach

1 🔘 MAP 128, B1

Northleach, 9 miles west of Burford, has been a small market town since 1227, but remains refreshingly uncommercialised. The grandeur and complexity of its **Church of St Peter & St Paul** (www.northleach.org; Church Walk; ⊙9am-5pm), a masterpiece of the Cotswold Perpendicular style, testifies to its wool-era wealth.

Late-medieval cottages, imposing merchants' stores and half-timbered Tudor houses jostle for position in a wonderful melange of styles around Market Sq. One 17th-century wool house holds the hugely enjoyable **Mechanical Music Museum** (☏01451-860181; www.mechanicalmusic.co.uk; High St; adult/child £8/3.50; ⊙10am-5pm), a quirky collection of antique music players. Join an hour-long tour to hear some truly amazing sounds;

the front room is a cosy licensed café, so you can have a drink as you wait for the next tour.

To learn more about regional history, ecology, traditions and attractions, call in at the **Cotswolds Discovery Centre** (Escape to the Cotswolds; ☏01451-861563; www.cotswoldsaonb.org.uk; Fosse Way; admission free; ⊙9.30am-4pm Thu-Mon; P), in the Old Prison at the northwest end of town.

Lively, stylish and laid-back, **Wheatsheaf** (☏01451-860244; www.cotswoldswheatsheaf.com; West End; mains £14.50-24; ⊙8-10am, noon-3pm & 6-9pm Mon-Thu & Sun, to 10pm Fri & Sat; P 🛜 👬) is a beautifully revamped coaching inn where diners dig into excellent, elegant seasonal British dishes with a contemporary kick. It's a huge local hit. The inventive, unpretentious menu delights with seasonal risottos, shellfish, richly flavoured pies, succulent steaks and some tempting sides, along

Chedworth Roman Villa

Rediscovered by a Victorian gamekeeper in 1864, the impressive **Chedworth Roman Villa** (Map p128, A1; NT; ☏01242-890256; www.nationaltrust.org.uk; Yanworth; adult/child £10.50/5.25; ⊙10am-5pm Apr-Oct, to 4pm mid-Feb–Mar & Nov; P) stands in a surprisingly out-of-the-way location, at the far end of a dead-end rural road, 4.5 miles west of Northleach and signposted from the A429.

The earliest section of this large and luxurious private residence dates to around AD 175. It was at its most magnificent, though, around AD 362, equipped with two sets of bathhouses, a water shrine and a dining room with underfloor heating. A fine modern gallery preserves several exquisite mosaics, though yet more, unearthed recently, had to be re-buried due to lack of resources.

Oxford Brush Company

Yes, the only thing the **Oxford Brush Company** (📞01993-824148; www.oxfordbrushcompany.com; 54 High St, Burford; ⏰9.30am-5.30pm Mon-Sat, 10am-5pm Sun) sells is brushes. But they are very nice brushes, the kind of brushes you might buy even if you didn't think you needed a brush. Perhaps a nailbrush? A clothes brush? Or just a brush to clean your other brushes?

with all-essential aperitifs and complimentary sparkling water. It also has fabulous old-meets-new rooms upstairs.

Bibury

2 ◎ MAP 128, B2

Memorably described as 'England's most beautiful village' by no less an authority than William Morris, Bibury, 10 miles southwest

of Burford towards Cirencester, epitomises the Cotswolds at its most picturesque. With its cluster of perfect cottages beside the River Coln, and tangle of narrow flower-lined lanes, small wonder that it's a major halt on large-group Cotswold tours.

The big attraction is **Arlington Row**, a ravishing set of rustic cottages that was originally a 14th-century wool store, before being converted into workers' lodgings. Seen in movies like Stardust – and on the inside front cover of UK passports – the houses overlook marshy Rack Isle, a low-lying area once used to dry cloth and graze cattle, and now a wildlife refuge.

Bibury's central, Saxon-built **Church of St Mary the Virgin** (Church Rd; ⏰10am-dusk) has been much altered since its original construction, but many 8th-century features are still visible among the 12th-, 13th- and 15th-century additions.

Kelmscott Manor

Nestling near the Thames, 10 miles south of Burford, **Kelmscott Manor** (Map p128, E4; 📞01367-252486; www.sal.org.uk/kelmscott-manor; Kelmscott; adult/child £10/5; ⏰11am-5pm Wed & Sat Apr-Oct) is a gorgeous garden-fringed Tudor pile that was bought in 1871 by a prestigious pair of artist-poets: Dante Gabriel Rossetti and William Morris, founder of the Arts and Crafts movement. The interior is true to Morris' philosophy that one should own nothing that is neither beautiful nor useful, and displays his personal effects along with fabrics and furniture designed by Morris and his associates.

Minster Lovell Hall

Minster Lovell

3 ◉ MAP 128, F2

In the gorgeous, flower-filled village of Minster Lovell, 6 miles east of Burford and barely changed since medieval times, a clutch of thatch-roofed stone cottages nestles beside an ancient pub and riverside mill.

The main local sight is **Minster Lovell Hall** (EH; www.english-herit age.org.uk; Old Minster; admission free; ⏱24hr), a 15th-century riverside manor house that fell into ruins after being abandoned in 1747. Richard III stayed here in 1483, and its owner Viscount Francis Lovell fought alongside him at the Battle of Bosworth two years later. You can pass through the vaulted porch to peek past blackened walls into its roofless great hall, interior courtyard and crumbling tower, while the wind whistles through the gaping windows.

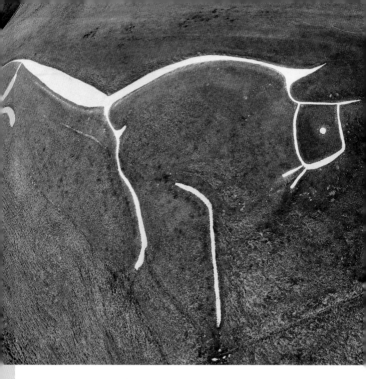

Worth a Trip 🔭
Vale of the White Horse

The verdant Vale of the White Horse, 20 miles southwest of Oxford, is home to the historic market town of Wantage, birthplace of Alfred the Great (AD 849–899). Its most interesting attractions, however, are much older even than that. White Horse Hill, 7.5 miles west of Wantage, is decorated with Britain's most ancient chalk figure, the Uffington White Horse, while other similarly ancient sites stand nearby.

www.nationaltrust.org.uk

White Horse Hill

admission free

⊙ dawn-dusk

There's no public transport. The site car park is 7.5 miles west of Wantage, signposted off the B4507.

Uffington White Horse

On the lower slopes of its high namesake hill, a half-mile walk east through the fields from the hillside car park, the elegant, minimalist Uffington White Horse (pictured) is the oldest chalk figure in Britain. Created during the Bronze Age around 3000 years ago by cutting 1m-deep trenches out of the hill and filling them with blocks of chalk, it has been maintained by locals for centuries. Perhaps it was a display for the gods; it's best seen from the air.

Uffington Castle

Uffington Castle, atop White Horse Hill, is a superbly sited hill fort that dates from around 700 BC. All that's visible today is the vast grassed-over earthen wall that once surrounded it, enclosing large, long-vanished wooden huts. This is Oxfordshire's highest point (262m), so views stretch in every direction.

Dragon Hill

The 10m-high, flat-topped mound known as Dragon Hill sits just below the outline of the White Horse, off the B4507. In local lore, this was the site where St George slew the dragon. Archaeologists believe it's a natural formation, the summit of which was scraped level during the Iron Age, and used for rituals.

Wayland's Smithy

Much older even than the nearby White Horse, Wayland's Smithy is a chambered neolithic long barrow, 1.4 miles southwest of the car park, which measures over 50m long. Fourteen skeletons discovered within were interred more than 5000 years ago, by which time the 87-mile Ridgeway path on which it stands was already in use. Sadly, its impressive entrance is sealed, so you can't explore inside.

★ **Top Tips**

All the sites on White Horse Hill are administered by the National Trust (www.nationaltrust.org.uk), and are accessible free of charge from dawn to dusk.

✕ **Take A Break**

The main square in Wantage holds several chain cafes and restaurants. In Woolstone, a mile north of White Horse Hill, an attractive, half-timbered 500-year-old pub, the **White Horse** (☎ 01367-820726; www.whitehorse-woolstone.co.uk; Woolstone; ☺ 8-10am, noon-2.30pm & 6-9pm), serves good modern food, including fresh fish and vegetarian options like cashew-nut curry.

Explore

Cirencester & the Southwest Cotswolds

Charming Cirencester (siren-sester), as Corinium, was England's second city under the Romans. Medieval trade brought further prosperity, and the construction of a superb church. Today's Cirencester is elegant and affluent but unpretentious. Upmarket boutiques and delis line its narrow streets, while beautiful Victorian buildings flank the central square.

Spend half a day in Cirencester, visiting the Corinium Museum (p137) and huge St John the Baptist's Church (p137), and dining perhaps in Jesse's Bistro (p137). Then head for delightful Painswick and its unique Rococo Garden (p141), calling in at the nearby Woolpack Inn. A second day hereabouts can take you to Uley and its prehistoric sites (p142), and Tetbury (p142), home to royal Highgrove.

Getting There & Around

🚌 Buses link Cirencester with Northleach (route 855; £2.90, 20 minutes), Tetbury (route 882; £2.70, 30 minutes) and London (£6, 2½ hours), while Stroud is connected with Painswick (route 66; £2.20, seven minutes), Tetbury (route 69; £2.70, 40 minutes) and Uley (route 65; £3.80, 35 minutes).

🚉 The closest station to Cirencester, at Kemble 4.5 miles south, is connected with London Paddington (£28.10, 1¼ hours).

Cirencester & the Southwest Cotswolds Map p140

Street scene, Cirencester (p136) MILOSZ MASLANKA / SHUTTERSTOCK ©

Top Sights 📷
Cirencester

Cirencester today is both elegant and affluent, but refreshingly unpretentious. Upmarket boutiques and fashionable delis now line its narrow streets, but its Monday and Friday markets remain at the core of its identity. Beautiful Victorian buildings flank the busy central square, while the surrounding streets showcase a harmonious medley of historic architecture.

◉ MAP P140, E2

Cirencester is easy to reach from London or Bristol, standing 20 miles northwest along the A419 from Swindon on the M4, and it's also 16 miles south of Cheltenham.

Corinium Museum

Most of this wonderful modern **museum** (📞01285-655611; www.coriniummuseum.org; Park St; adult/child £5.60/2.70; ⏰10am-5pm Mon-Sat, 2-5pm Sun Apr-Oct, to 4pm Nov-Mar; 👤) is, of course, dedicated to Cirencester's Roman past; reconstructed rooms, videos and interactive displays bring the era to life. Among the highlights are some beautiful floor mosaics (pictured, left), unearthed locally and including a 4th-century mosaic depicting the mythical lyre-player Orpheus charming animals, and the 2nd-century 'Jupiter column', a carved capital depicting Bacchus and his drunken mates. There's also an excellent Anglo-Saxon section, plus exhibits on medieval Cirencester and its prosperous wool trade.

St John the Baptist's Church

One of England's largest parish churches, the cathedral-like **St John's** (pictured p136; 📞01285-659317; www.cirenparish.co.uk; Market Sq; ⏰10am-4pm) boasts an outstanding Perpendicular Gothic tower with flying buttresses (c 1400), plus a majestic three-storey south porch, built as an office in the late 15th century but subsequently used as Cirencester's town hall. Soaring arches, magnificent fan vaulting and a Tudor nave adorn the light-filled interior, where a wall safe holds the Boleyn Cup, made for Anne Boleyn in 1535.

Amphitheatre

Very little now remains of Corinium, but you can still admire the (very) grassed-over contours of the **amphitheatre** (EH; www.english-heritage.org.uk; Cotswold Ave; admission free; ⏰dawn-dusk), one of the largest in the country, beside Bristol Rd on the western side of town. Dating back to the early 2nd century AD, it held space for 8000 spectators. Access is via Cotswold Ave.

✕ Take a Break

Jesse's Bistro (www.jessesbistro.co.uk; The Stableyard, 14 Black Jack St; mains £16-28; ⏰11.45am-2.45pm Mon, 11.45am-2.45pm & 6.45-9.45pm Tue-Sat, 11.45am-4.45pm Sun) is a pleasant spot serving dishes fresh from the semi-open kitchen.

Made by Bob (www.foodmadebybob.com; Corn Hall, 26 Market Pl; mains £8.50-22.50; ⏰7.30am-5pm Mon-Sat, from 10am Sun; 👤) is part deli, part brasserie, and popular for its casual atmosphere.

New Brewery Arts Cafe (www.newbreweryarts.org.uk; Brewery Ct; mains £6-8.50; ⏰9am-5pm Mon-Sat, 10am-4pm Sun; 📶👤👤) is a friendly daytime-only cafe, on the upper level of Cirencester's lively arts centre, serving breakfast or lunch.

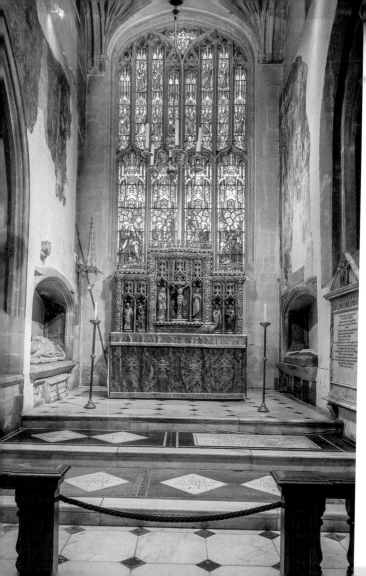

New Brewery Arts

At this very central converted Victorian **brewery** (☎01285-657181; www.newbreweryarts.org.uk; Brewery Ct; admission free; ☺9am-5pm Mon-Sat, 9.30am-4pm Sun), you can pop in to over a dozen craft studios and observe jewellers, sculptors, glassblowers and so on at work. You can also see exhibitions in the main gallery and attend workshops and classes, ranging from creative writing to ceramics and photography. It also holds a good hostel and cafe (p137).

Cirencester Park

Unusually for a stately home, the mansion of the Earl of Bathurst sits right on the western edge of town, hidden by what's said to be Britain's tallest yew hedge. It's off-limits to visitors, but the extensive landscaped **grounds** (☎01865-653135; www.cirencesterpark.co.uk; Cecily Hill; admission free; ☺8am-5pm) that lie behind make a lovely spot for a stroll.

View of St John the Baptist's Church (p137)

Cirencester & the Southwest Cotswolds

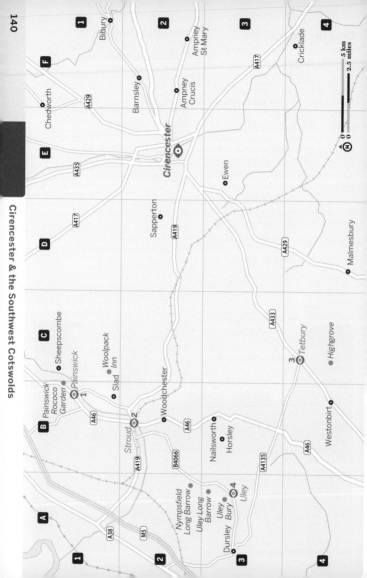

1
2
3
4

A
B
C
D
E
F

Bibury

Ampney
St Mary

Cricklade

Chedworth

Barnsley

A429

Ampney
Crucis

A417

Cirencester

A435

A417

Ewen

Sapperton

A419

Malmesbury

A429

Sheepscombe

Painswick
Rococo
Garden

Painswick

Woolpack
Inn

Slad

Woodchester

A46

Stroud

A419

A46

A433

Tetbury

Highgrove

Nailsworth

Horsley

Westonbirt

B4066

Nympsfield
Long Barrow

Uley Long
Barrow

Uley
Bury

Uley

A4135

A46

Dursley

A38

M5

N

0   5 km
0   2.5 miles

Painswick

1 ◉ MAP P140, B1

The beautiful and unspoiled hilltop village of Painswick sits on the Cotswold Way, 15 miles northwest of Cirencester. Wander its narrow winding streets to admire picture-perfect cottages, handsome stone houses and medieval inns.

A fine 14th-century, Perpendicular Gothic wool church, **St Mary's Church** (www.beaconbenefice.org.uk/painswick; New St; ⏱9.30am-dusk), stands in the centre, surrounded by 18th-century tabletop tombs and clipped yew trees sculpted to resemble giant ice lollies.

The unique **Painswick Rococo Garden** (Map p140, B1; 📞01452-813204; www.rococogarden.org.uk; off B4073; adult/child £7.50/3.60; ⏱10.30am-5pm mid-Jan–Oct; P 🚼) is half a mile north of the village. England's only such garden to survive, it was laid out by Benjamin Hyett in the 1740s as a vast 'outdoor room'. Restored to its original glory, it's absolutely stunning. Winding paths soften its geo-metrical precision, leading visitors to Gothic follies that include the eccentric Red House, where Latin quotes from the Song of Solomon are etched into the stained-glass windows.

Behind a soft-gold stone facade, the elegantly laid-back **Falcon** (📞01452-814222; www.falconpainswick.co.uk; New St; mains £12-24; ⏱noon-2.30pm & 6.30-9.30pm Mon-Sat, noon-3pm & 6.30-9pm Sun; 🛜) specialises in smartly presented, season-inspired British-European fare. Cheery staff deliver crisp salads, soups and sharing cheese platters, plus a varied selection of elaborate mains that might include risotto, lasagne, ale pie, roast lamb or stuffed trout.

Run by a charming Colombian couple – yes, the coffee's first-rate – **Olivas** (📞01452-814774; www.olivas.moonfruit.com; Friday St; mains £6-11; ⏱10am-5pm; 🛜) is a welcoming little backstreet cafe-deli that's a social hub for Painswick. Linger over a lunchtime stew or Spanish-style tapas at one of the tiny street-front tables, or pick up the perfect hiker's picnic.

Cider with Laurie

Bucolic little **Slad**, 2 miles south of Painswick in the Slad Valley, was the much-loved home of writer Laurie Lee (1914–97), who immortalised its beauty in *Cider with Rosie*. Lee's portrait and books adorn the walls of his lively local pub, the **Woolpack Inn** (Map p140, C1; 📞01452-813429; www.thewoolpackslad.com; Slad; mains £12-19; ⏱noon-11pm Sun & Mon, to midnight Tue-Thu, to 1am Fri & Sat, food served 6-9pm Mon, noon-3pm & 6-9pm Tue-Sat, noon-4pm Sun; 🍽), which serves excellent local beers and, of course, Cotswold Cider.

Stroud

2 ⊙ MAP P140, B2

A sizeable town by Cotswolds standards, Stroud, 15 miles west of Cirencester, once hummed with the sound of more than 150 cloth mills in action, but when the bottom fell out of the industry it went into decline. Now something of a bohemian enclave, known for its fair-trade shops, independent stores and lively arts scene, Stroud is not really a tourist destination, but it's still one of the Cotswolds' most important market towns, with dozens of stallholders converging for the weekly Saturday farmers market.

Local produce plays a prominent part in the inventive, mostly vegetarian dishes whipped up at bubbly **Star Anise** (☎01453-840021; www.staranisartscafe.com; Gloucester St; mains £6-9; ⊗8am-5pm Mon-Sat; 🛜🖼). Tuck into lunchtime soups, pastas, felafel and hummus platters, or delicious breakfasts, homemade cakes, freshly baked bread and Bristol-roasted coffee. It often hosts live music and other creative events.

Tetbury

3 ⊙ MAP P140, C4

Once a prosperous wool-trading centre, Tetbury, 10 miles southwest of Cirencester, is an appealing town where the busy streets are lined with medieval cottages, sturdy old townhouses and Geor-gian gems. The central square hosts markets every Wednesday and Saturday; look out for the 17th-century **Market House** (Market Pl), perched on stone pillars that seem to bulge under its weight.

A mile southwest of Tetbury, **Highgrove** (Map p140, C4; ☎0303 123 7310; www.highgrovegardens.com; Doughton; tours £27.50; ⊗Apr-Sep; 🅿), the private residence of Prince Charles and the Duchess of Cornwall, is famous for its exquisite, sustainable, organic gardens, which include rows of shape-clipped yews and a 'carpet garden' modelled on an oriental rug. Two-hour garden tours run on select summer days, and usually sell out far in advance.

Uley

4 ⊙ MAP P140, A3

This lovely little hamlet, 18 miles west of Cirencester, boasts a quaint village green and jumble of pretty houses. A steep footpath climbs from the village church to the overgrown remains of England's largest Iron Age hill fort, **Uley Bury** (Map p140, A3; admission free; ⊗24hr; 🅿), dating from around 300 BC. A 1.1-mile perimeter track leads around its ramparts, with fabulous views over Uley and the Severn Vale.

Just over a mile north, the much older **Uley Long Barrow** (Hetty Pegler's Tump; EH; Map p140, A3; www.english-heritage.org.uk; B4066; admission free; ⊗24hr) is a well-

Shopping

Stroud plays host to the greatest of all Cotswold farmers markets every Saturday 9am to 2pm. Dozens of stallholders converge on Cornhill Market Pl and the surrounding streets to sell everything from homemade soaps and Cotswolds ceramics to fresh local produce such as meat, cheese, cakes, bread and wine.)

A flower-scented dream in the very centre of Tetbury, **Highgrove Shop** (☑01666-505666; www.highgroveshop.com; 10 Long St; ☺9.30am-5pm Mon-Sat, 10.30am-4.30pm Sun) is the perfect spot to pick up candles, mugs, jams, treats, gardening trinkets and gorgeous homeware inspired by Prince Charles' sustainable gardens at nearby Highgrove.

preserved 37m-long chambered neolithic burial mound that was constructed around 3500 BC. Since the first archaeological digs in the late 19th century, around 15 interments have been unearthed here.

In a spectacular hilltop location another mile north along the Cotswold Way, **Nympsfield Long Barrow** (EH; Map p140, A2; www.english-heritage.org.uk; B4066; admission free; ☺24hr; ☑) is a 5000-year-old oval-shaped earth mound. Successive excavations have uncovered at least 13 human skeletons, along with fragments of neolithic pottery, inside its burial chambers, which now lie partly exposed.

A romantic vision of the English country pub, nestled on the village green with whitewashed walls and a snug interior, the **Old Crown Inn** (☑01453-860502; www.theoldcrownuley.co.uk; 17 The Green; mains £7-12; ☺noon-2pm & 6-9pm Mon-Fri, noon-9pm Sat & Sun; ☑ 🕭 🐾) serves old-fashioned meals – ham and chips, steak and ale pie, ploughman's lunches – at old-fashioned prices, plus a fine selection of local beers and ciders. It also has four simple en-suite rooms upstairs (double including breakfast from £75).

Survival Guide

All Souls College (p48), Oxford DAVID IONUT / SHUTTERSTOCK ©

Before You Go

Book Your Stay

Oxford has a limited supply of visitor accommodation. It's always hard to find a decent double room for under £100, and you can easily pay double that in summer.

The city centre is Oxford's most appealing neighbourhood, but it's so dense with historic buildings that it only holds a handful of hotels and B&Bs. Oxford's cheaper hotels tend to range along the main roads into town, while smaller-scale B&Bs are scattered through residential neighbourhoods.

There's a cluster of hostels close to Oxford's main train station, a few minutes' walk west of the centre.

The Cotswolds boast plenty of high-end, honey-hued country-house hotels, but few budget alternatives. Village pubs

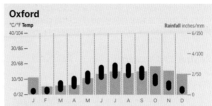

Oxford

When to Go

• **Winter** (Dec–Feb) The wettest and coldest months, with some snow and ice. Oxford hunkers down, and the Cotswolds are quiet.

• **Spring** (Mar–May) A lovely time to stroll in the Cotswolds or hike in the Cotswolds, with temperatures rising and blossom appearing.

• **Summer** (Jun–Aug) Prime tourist season, with daily highs exceeding 20°C. The Cotswolds are crowded, while Oxford empties of students.

• **Autumn** (Sep–Nov) Autumn delights in the Cotswolds, and Oxford buzzes with the new term, but rain often arrives in November.

are the best bet for good-value rooms.

In Oxford and the Cotswolds alike, booking ahead is strongly recommended, especially during weekends and the May-to-September high season.

Useful Websites

Lonely Planet (www.lonelyplanet.com/england/oxfordshire/oxford/hotels) Recommendations and bookings.

Oxford Tourist Office (www.experienceoxfordshire.org) Accommodation bookings for visitors, either in person or by phone, for a small fee.

University Rooms Oxford (www.universityrooms.com) Rooms in colleges and other student accommodation, during university holidays.

Best Budget Oxford

Oxford YHA (www.yha.org.uk) Much the best

of Oxford's hostels – albeit not the cheapest – this new-built YHA is right beside the station.

Central Backpackers (www.centralbackpackers.co.uk) In the finest tradition of friendly, low-cost hostels for international travellers.

Oxford Backpackers (www.hostels.co.uk) If price is your main priority, this basic option can't be beat.

Best Midrange Oxford

Tower House (www.towerhouseoxford.co.uk) Charming, friendly and great-value central accommodation in a 17th-century townhouse; profits go to community causes.

Remont (www.remont-oxford.co.uk) Rates in this boutique guesthouse are such a bargain because it's 2.5 miles north of the centre.

Richmond Hotel (☎01865-311777) Jericho's best-value option, close to the action above a Lebanese restaurant.

Galaxie Hotel (www.galaxie.co.uk) This

smart B&B inn, 1.5 miles north of the centre, offers excellent rates.

Best Top End Oxford

Head of the River (www.headoftheriveroxford.co.uk) Stylish rooms in a riverfront warehouse, above an excellent pub and overlooking the Thames.

Malmaison Oxford Castle (www.malmaison.com) Guests in this upscale hotel, in a historic castle tower, sleep in plush converted prison cells.

Holywell B&B (www.holywellbedandbreakfast.com) Delightful and very welcoming two-room B&B, in a charming 500-year-old cottage on a peaceful central street.

Oxford Coach & Horses (www.oxfordcoachandhorses.co.uk) A bright modern makeover has turned this old coaching inn, east of the centre, into a boutique gem.

Best in the Cotswolds

Barnsley House (www.barnsleyhouse.com)

Lavish and irresistibly romantic hotel in a 17th-century country house, set in beautiful gardens 4 miles northeast of Cirencester.

Painswick (www.thepainswick.co.uk) Chic and very dramatic hotel, right in the middle of Painswick village, with grand and stylish rooms and a high-class restaurant.

Falkland Arms (www.falklandarms.co.uk) This venerable thatched pub, the centrepiece of the pretty village of Great Tew, 6 miles east of Chipping Norton, offers great-value rooms and good food.

YHA Cotswolds (www.yha.org.uk) The only YHA hostel in the Cotswolds, a spanking new, environmentally super-aware affair, forms part of a vibrant arts centre in the middle of Cirencester.

Wheatsheaf (www.cotswoldswheatsheaf.com) Historic coaching inn on the main street of Northleach, with seductive and classy accommodation and a dazzling modern dining room.

Star Cottage (www. burfordbedandbreak fast.co.uk) Two lovely B&B rooms in a cosy rural cottage, a mile northeast of Burford.

No 12 (www.no12 cirencester.co.uk) Friendly Cirencester town house with four secluded and attractively furnished B&B rooms plus a very pleasant garden.

Arriving in Oxford

Heathrow Airport

The closest airport to Oxford, London Heathrow, is 43 miles southeast of Oxford, and 15 miles west of London. There are no direct trains to Oxford from Heathrow; rail passengers have to travel via London. A round-the-clock bus service, however, 'The Airline', run by **Oxford Bus Company** (☎01865-785400; www.ox fordbus.co.uk), connects Gloucester Green in Oxford with Heathrow every 20 to 30 minutes in daytime, and less

frequently through the night (£23, 1½ hours).

Gatwick Airport

London's Gatwick airport is 75 miles southeast of Oxford. While rail passengers have to change trains in either Reading or London, 'The Airline' bus links Oxford's Gloucester Green with Gatwick hourly in daytime, and every two hours at night (£28, two to 2½ hours).

Oxford Station

Oxford's main train station is conveniently located just west of the city centre, roughly 10 minutes' walk from major attractions. To walk into the centre, head east along Park End St to reach High St, or fork left onto Hythe Bridge St for Broad St. Buses X13 and X3 run to High St, while bus 5 runs through the centre, via St Aldate's, and continues southeast along Cowley Rd. Taxis are available.

Oxford Parkway

Oxford Parkway station, on Banbury Rd 4 miles north of the

centre, is served by trains from London Marylebone (£7 to £26, one hour). The Park & Ride 500 bus connects the station with the city centre, as well as Oxford's main rail and bus stations.

Oxford Bus Station

Oxford's chaotic outdoor bus station is on the northwestern edge of the centre, on Gloucester Green near the corner of Worcester and George Sts. To reach anywhere in central Oxford, it's quickest to walk, but taxis are also available.

Getting Around

Bicycle

Cycling is the perfect way to get around Oxford. **Cyclo Analysts** (www.cycloanalysts. com) and **Summertown Cycles** (www. summertowncycles. co.uk) sell, repair and rent out bikes, including hybrids.

The Cotswolds are a popular destination for cycle tours. Each village is comfortably close to the next, and the terrain is seldom demanding.

Bus

Oxford's busy and wide-ranging network of local buses is operated by Oxford Bus Company and **Stagecoach** (www.stagecoachbus.com).

Single journeys within Oxford cost up to £2.20 (return £3.70); consider a day pass (£4.20). Pay when you board the bus, either in cash or with a contactless card.

Several bus companies connect the Cotswolds villages. As services tend to be infrequent, and most routes don't operate on Sundays, travelling by bus in the Cotswolds requires careful planning and patience.

The **Cotswolds Discoverer** (adult/child £10/5), a great-value one-day pass that gives unlimited travel on bus or train routes throughout the region,

can be bought at all UK mainline train stations, and aboard participating buses within the Cotswolds.

Cotswold Green (📞01453-835153) Serves the southern Cotswolds, including Cirencester, Stroud and Tetbury.

Johnsons Excelbus (www.johnsons coaches.co.uk) Links Broadway, Chipping Campden and Moreton-in-Marsh with Stratford-upon-Avon.

Marchants (www.marchants-coaches.com) Focuses on the northern Cotswolds, connecting Broadway, Chipping Campden and Winchcombe.

Pulhams (www.pulhamscoaches.com) Runs throughout the Cotswolds.

Stagecoach (www.stagecoachbus.com) Operates throughout the Cotswolds, and also links Oxford with Blenheim Palace, Burford and Chipping Norton.

Swanbrook (www.swanbrook.co.uk) Offers services to Burford, Minster Lovell and Northleach.

Car & Motorcycle

A car or motorcycle is the most flexible way to explore the Cotswolds, or to reach rural pubs and restaurants, but it's a liability within Oxford city centre.

Much of central Oxford is pedestrianised, and traffic moves very slowly. Little parking is available, with on-street parking limited to two hours in daytime. The largest central car park, at the Westgate Shopping Centre, charges £25 for overnight parking.

If you drive to Oxford, use one of the five **Park & Ride** sites (www.oxford.gov.uk) around the perimeter, roughly 2 miles out. These typically charge £6.80 per day for a vehicle and all passengers, including the return bus trip into town.

Train

Trains are not a viable way to explore the Cotswolds, but a couple of towns in the region are accessible by rail.

Moreton-in-Marsh is served by direct trains from Oxford (£10.60, 35 minutes) and London Paddington (£14.50, 1½ hours).

Stroud is connected by direct trains to London Paddington (£28.10, 1½ hours), which also call at Kemble, 4½ miles south of Cirencester.

Around five steam or heritage diesel trains run daily excursions in summer between Cheltenham and Broadway, via Winchcombe, on the **Gloucestershire Warwickshire Railway** (www.gwsr.com; return fare £18).

Essential Information

Accessible Travel

All new buildings have wheelchair access, and many hotels, restaurants and sights in grand older buildings have lifts, ramps and other facilities. However, some hotels, B&Bs, restaurants and attractions in smaller

historic properties have proved harder to adapt.

Download Lonely Planet's free Accessible Travel guides from http://lptravel.to/AccessibleTravel.

Public Transport

All Oxford's city buses are wheelchair-accessible, and **Oxford Cars** (☏01865-406070; www.oxfordcars.co.uk) offers taxis that can accommodate wheelchairs on demand.

The main long-distance operator, **National Express** (☏0871-7818181; www.nationalexpress.com), has wheelchair-friendly coaches on many routes.

A Disabled Person's Railcard (www.disabledpersons-railcard.co.uk) costs £20 and gets 33% off most train fares for you and a friend.

Useful Resources

Accessible Oxford Guide (www.experienceoxfordshire.org) A link on the tourist office's homepage (under 'Plan Your Trip') connects to this compre-

hensive, downloadable 72-page guide to Oxford for disabled travellers.

Disability Rights UK (www.disabilityrights uk.org) Sells a Holiday Guide and a key to public disabled toilets.

Shopmobility (www.westgateoxford.co.uk) The Westgate Shopping Centre supplies free wheelchairs and scooters from a base in its car park, for use throughout the city centre.

Tourism For All (www.tourismforall.org.uk) Provides personalised information for disabled travellers. Annual fee of £25 for UK residents; £40 for those from overseas.

Business Hours

Opening hours for sights and activities vary throughout the year. Many operate shorter hours from October to March; some shut down altogether during the winter.

Banks 9.30am to 4pm or 5pm Monday to Friday; possibly 9.30am to 1pm Saturday.

Oxford Colleges All colleges are liable to close to visitors for special events, or simply at the whim of their all-powerful porters. Several only allow visitors for two or three hours in the afternoon.

Pubs and bars Noon to 11pm Monday to Saturday (some until midnight or up to 3am Friday and Saturday), 12.30pm to 11pm Sunday.

Restaurants Lunch: noon to 2.30pm or 3pm; dinner: 6pm to 9pm or 10pm.

Shops 9am to 5.30pm or 6pm Monday to Saturday, normally 11am to 5pm Sunday.

Dangers & Annoyances

Oxford is generally a safe town, but crime does exist.

○ Central Oxford is so compact that even if you walk everywhere, there's no real risk of wandering into unsafe areas.

○ Take care if you're out late in the city centre, especially on Friday and Saturday nights when the pubs and clubs are emptying; ongoing 'town versus gown' tensions can provoke confrontations.

Discount Cards

There are no specific discount cards for Oxford visitors, but if you have a student identity card of some kind you'll be able to benefit from reduced rates at many local attractions and businesses.

Electricity

Type G
230V/50Hz

Emergency Numbers

Emergency (police, fire, ambulance)	☏ 999 (or 112)

Etiquette

○ **College names** Some Oxford colleges are always referred to by their

full names, while others are not. Thus it's always 'Christ Church' rather than 'Christ Church College', but never 'New' instead of 'New College'. Try to follow local practice.

○ **Queues** In England, queuing ('standing in line') is sacrosanct, whether to board a bus, buy tickets or enter an attraction. Any attempt to 'jump the queue' will result in an outburst of tut-tutting and hard stares.

Insurance

Although everyone in England receives free emergency medical treatment, regardless of nationality, travel insurance is still highly recommended. It usually covers medical and dental consultation and treatment at private clinics, which can be quicker than NHS places, as well as the cost of any emergency flights – plus all the usual stuff like loss of baggage.

Worldwide travel insurance is available at www.lonelyplanet.com/travel-insurance. You can buy, extend and claim online any-time – even if you're already on the road.

Internet Access

o 3G and 4G mobile broadband coverage is good in Oxford and the major Cotswold towns, but beware potentially high charges for data roaming – check with your provider before travelling.

o All hotels, B&Bs and hostels in Oxford, all hotels and village inns in the Cotswolds, and most cafes and coffee shops, have wi-fi access, usually free. This widespread access means internet cafes are scarce.

o **Oxford County Library**, on Queensgate, has free wi-fi and inter-net access (30 minutes maximum if busy), plus sockets for charging devices.

LGBT+ Travellers

Although Oxford is, like most English cities these days, a generally tolerant place for LGB-TIQ travellers, it has a surprisingly small gay scene. Restaurants, nightspots and accom-modation providers are very unlikely to

have an issue with your sexuality, but you might still find pockets of homophobic hostil-ity elsewhere.

Resources include the following:

Diva (www.divamag. co.uk)

Gay Oxford (www.gay oxford.co.uk) A limited guide to Oxford's gay nightlife.

Gay Times (www. gaytimes.co.uk)

LGBT+ Oxford (www. lgbtoxon.uk) Website with links to community resources and events.

Pink Times Oxford (www.facebook.com/ PinkTimesOxford) Twice-yearly magazine covering gay life in Oxfordshire.

Switchboard LGBT+ Helpline (www.switch board.lgbt; ☎0300 330 0630)

Money
ATMs

ATMs (popularly known 'cash ma-chines') are common in Oxford, while all but the very tiniest Cotswolds towns hold at least one. Most are free to use (look for the 'free cash' sign),

but some, inside shops for example, charge a small fee for withdraw-als. If you're not from the UK, your home bank will likely charge you for withdrawing money overseas.

Cash

The currency of Britain is the pound sterling (£). Paper money (notes) comes in £5, £10, £20 and £50 denominations. Some shops don't accept £50 notes because fakes circulate.

Other currencies are very rarely accepted.

Credit & Debit Cards

Visa and MasterCard are widely accepted, though some smaller B&Bs may take cash only. Other credit cards, including Amex, may not be accepted. Most businesses will assume that your card is 'Chip and PIN' enabled; if it isn't, you should be able to sign instead, but some places may not accept it. Many businesses – and Oxford's local buses – encourage customers to use 'contactless' card payments rather than cash for small purchases.

Taxes & Refunds

Value-added tax (VAT), a sales tax that's charged on most purchases at 20%, is always included in quoted prices. At time of writing, non-EU residents can reclaim the VAT on certain purchased goods; see www.gov.uk/tax-on-shopping/taxfree-shopping for further details.

Tipping

o **Pubs & Bars** Not expected if you order drinks (or food) and pay at the bar; usually 10% if you order at the table and your meal is brought to you.

o **Restaurants** Around 10% in restaurants and cafes with table service, 15% at smarter restaurants. Tips may be added to your bill as a 'service charge' – it's not compulsory to pay.

o **Taxis** Usually 10%, or rounded up to the nearest pound.

Post

Britain's postal services are generally reliable. Oxford's main **post office** (102 St Aldate's; ⏰9am-5.30pm Mon & Wed-Sat, from 9.30am Tue) is in the city centre. For information on Cotswolds locations, and on postal rates, visit www.postoffice.co.uk.

Public Holidays

Oxford and the Cotswolds observe the same holidays as the rest of England:

New Year's Day 1 January

Easter March/April (Good Friday to Easter Monday inclusive)

May Day First Monday in May

Spring Bank Holiday Last Monday in May

Summer Bank Holiday Last Monday in August

Christmas Day 25 December

Boxing Day 26 December

Smoking

Smoking is forbidden in all enclosed public places in England. Most pubs have a smoking area outside. Vaping is a grey area – look out for signs.

Telephone

| Country code | ☎44 |
| International access code | ☎00 |

Mobile Phones

The UK uses the GSM 900/1800 network, which covers the rest of Europe, Australia and New Zealand, but isn't compatible with the North American GSM 1900. Most modern mobiles can function on both networks; check before you travel.

At time of writing, Europeans visiting the UK don't face roaming charges. Brexit might change that, so check before you leave.

Time

Greenwich Mean Time (UTC); in summer, British Summer Time (GMT+1).

Toilets

Public toilets in Oxford and the Cotswolds are generally clean and modern. Museums, bigger stores and railway stations also have facilities. Most public toilets are free, some charge a small fee. Pub and restaurant toilets tend to be for customer use only.

Tourist Information

Oxford's **Tourist Office** (☎01865-686430; www.experienceoxfordshire.org; 15-16 Broad St; ⏱9am-5.30pm Mon-Sat, 10am-4pm Sun Jul & Aug, 9.30am-5pm Mon-Sat, 10am-4pm Sun

Sep-Jun) covers the whole of Oxfordshire. It makes reservations for local accommodation and walking tours, and sells guidebooks plus tickets for events and attractions.

Most Cotswolds towns and villages have their own tourist offices. The **Cotswolds Discovery Centre** (Escape to the Cotswolds; ☎01451-861563; www.cotswoldsaonb.org.uk; Fosse Way, Northleach; ⏱9.30am-4pm Thu-Mon; **P**), the official

regional visitors centre in Northleach, is more useful for context than advice.

Volunteering

Oxfordshire Community and Voluntary Action (www.ocva.org.uk) connects would-be volunteers with organisations in need, and runs a monthly drop-in stall in the Westgate Centre if you'd like to discuss possibilities.

Behind the Scenes

Send Us Your Feedback

We love to hear from travellers – your comments help make our books better. We read every word, and we guarantee that your feedback goes straight to the authors. Visit lonelyplanet.com/contact to submit your updates and suggestions.

Note: We may edit, reproduce and incorporate your comments in Lonely Planet products such as guidebooks, websites and digital products, so let us know if you don't want your comments reproduced or your name acknowledged. For a copy of our privacy policy visit lonelyplanet.com/legal.

Greg's Thanks

Thanks to the many people who helped me as I pounded the streets of Oxford and criss-crossed the Cotswolds, and thanks especially to Adrian, Michael and Donald Ward for their Oxford memories and expertise. Thanks, too, to my editor Clifton Wilkinson for giving me this opportunity, and to my dear wife Sam for sharing so many adventures and late nights.

Acknowledgments

Cover photograph: Bridge of Sighs, Hertford College, Oxford, Alan Copson/AWL ©

Photographs p32 Joe Daniel Price/ Getty Images ©; p94 John Spreadbury/Shutterstock ©

This Book

This 1st edition of Lonely Planet's *Pocket Oxford & the Cotswolds* guidebook was researched and written by Greg Ward and Catherine Le Nevez, and curated by Greg. This guidebook was produced by the following:

Destination Editors Clifton Wilkinson, James Smart

Senior Product Editor Genna Patterson

Product Editor Bruce Evans

Senior Cartographer Mark Griffiths

Book Designer Meri Blazevski

Assisting Editors Imogen Bannister, Andrea Dobbin, Kristin Odijk

Assisting Cartographer Rachel Imeson

Cover Researcher Naomi Parker

Thanks to William Allen, Martine Power, Angela Tinson

Index

See also separate subindexes for:

⊗ **Eating p158**

⊕ **Drinking p158**

✿ **Entertainment p159**

🔒 **Shopping p159**

Sights 000
Map Pages **000**

⊗ Eating

Sights 000
Map Pages **000**

Our Writers

Greg Ward

Since whetting his appetite for travel by following the hippy trail to India, and later living in northern Spain, Greg Ward has written guides to destinations all over the world. As well as covering the USA from the Southwest to Hawaii, he has ranged on recent assignments from Corsica to the Cotswolds, and Japan to Corfu. See his website, www.gregward.info, for his favourite photos and memories.

Contributing Writer Catherine Le Nevez researched and wrote the Stratford-upon-Avon Worth a Trip feature.

Published by Lonely Planet Global Limited
CRN 554153
1st edition – Apr 2019
ISBN 978 1 78701 693 4
© Lonely Planet 2019   Photographs © as indicated 2019
10 9 8 7 6 5
Printed in Malaysia